CONNECTING

FAITH & WORK

IN THE 21ST CENTURY

CONNECTING
FAITH & WORK
IN THE 21ST CENTURY

Edited by Albert Erisman,
David Gill & Bill Peel

THEOLOGY OF WORK PROJECT

**Connecting Faith & Work in the 21st Century:
A Faith@Work Summit Study Guide**

Hendrickson Publishers Marketing, LLC
P.O. Box 3473
Peabody, Massachusetts 01961-3473
www.hendrickson.com

ISBN 978-1-61970-955-3

Printed in the United States of America

First Printing—October 2016

Contents

Preface

The leadership team for the 2014 Faith@Work Summit had its beginnings in a classroom at Gordon-Conwell Theological Seminary in 2011. The three of us had been on a long journey to connect our faith and our work, beginning in the 1970s. We had diverse careers, came from different educational backgrounds, and lived in different corners of the United States. Two of us (David Gill and Al Erisman) came together to lead a unique Gordon-Conwell Seminary program on Workplace Theology, Ethics, and Leadership. Bill Peel had decided to pursue his doctoral studies after a long workplace ministry career and was a part of that two-year program.

In 2012 David, director of Gordon-Conwell Theological Seminary's Mockler Center for Faith & Ethics in the Workplace, proposed a Faith@Work Summit Conference to the Kern Family Foundation, which quickly committed to a startup grant. He then approached Bill and Al to join him on a three-person organizing team. The three of us agreed together that this movement to connect Christian faith with work was growing, and it had little to do with any single individual leader or any one organization. It had everything to do with what God was doing not only in the United States but also throughout the world. We pondered the question: Wouldn't it be great if we could bring together a diverse collection of people to understand where we are with this movement and where it could go?

We had no interest in forming a new organization or creating a formal collaboration among existing organizations. It was evident that God was at work, and we simply wanted to catalyze a discussion, to provide encouragement, and to see if some sparks might produce a yet greater understanding of God's work in this area.

Not having an organization or seeking to push a particular point of view had advantages. The goal was to encourage a broad set of voices.

- Sometimes the work and faith movement has been associated with white-collar Christians in business, but we knew it was broader than that.

- As an independent activity, we didn't need to satisfy a particular organization, but we had the freedom to gather its many and varied voices.

- These voices did not have to bring the final word, or even to agree with one another. Each was valuable in provoking a richer understanding of what God was doing in workplaces around the world.

Not having an organization also had disadvantages. Pulling together the funding and organizational support required gaining support from many. David chaired and drove the process start to finish, but all three of us took on the tasks of shaping, encouraging, challenging, recruiting, fundraising, and so many other things. We met regularly for almost two years leading up to the summit.

We were extremely gratified that our own institutions (Gordon-Conwell Theological Seminary, Seattle Pacific University, and LeTourneau University) got behind the effort with some initial financial sponsorship, even under the conditions that the meeting would not shine a big light on these organizations and their work in the field. It was symbolic that the leadership represented a seminary, a business school, and an engineering school. Other organizations joined in the sponsorship, including the Kern Family Foundation, the H. E. Butt Family Foundation, and the Oikonomia Network. Many others also joined in and are listed in the Acknowledgments. David found a location that would accommodate what we optimistically thought would be a big gathering—around two hundred people. We finally had to close registration, though, more than a month before the summit in Boston, October 24–25, 2014. In the end, we had a room crammed with 280 enthusiastic people.

We also decided on the format for the summit: 16-minute short, focused talks on different aspects of the faith at work movement.

We wanted to encourage as broad a flavor as we could, and this format, rather than long plenaries, allowed that opportunity.

In this study guide, we provide overviews of the various talks, links to the 16-minute videos (which can be found at http://fwsummit.org/faithwork-summit-2014/), and study questions for small-group discussion. We also provide an extensive bibliography for further study. Also included are links to short tributes to five recent "pioneers" of the movement. We wanted to recognize those who laid the foundation for the uptick in activity. The closing Litany of Commitment was created by Bill and is included at the back of this study guide.

As we launch the second summit in Dallas, October 27–29, 2016, it is fitting to distribute this record of the first summit. God is at work through his people at work at this moment in the twenty-first century. It is a privilege to be able to join in his work.

Albert M. Erisman
Executive in Residence, School of Business,
Government, and Economics
Seattle Pacific University, Seattle, Washington

David W. Gill
Mockler-Phillips Professor of
Workplace Theology & Business Ethics
Director, Mockler Center for Faith & Ethics in the Workplace
Gordon-Conwell Theological Seminary,
South Hamilton, Massachusetts

Bill Peel
Executive Director, Center for Faith & Work
LeTourneau University, Longview, Texas

Acknowledgments

Yuna Oh, assistant to David Gill, played a vital role in her administrative and logistics work on the summit. Amanda Battaglia, working with Bill Peel, provided her expert abilities to create the look of the summit for the website, video screen, and conference workbook. Devin Marks coached each of the speakers. The aggressive schedule of multiple 16-minute talks would not have been possible without him.

The support of our institutions (Gordon-Conwell Theological Seminary, Seattle Pacific University, and LeTourneau University) is gratefully acknowledged. We are also grateful to lead sponsors for the summit: the Kern Family Foundation and the Howard E. Butt Foundation; and other sponsors, including Acton Institute, C12 New England, CBMC, The Gospel Coalition, The High Calling, Institute for Faith, Work & Economics, IVCF MBA Ministries, Marketplace Chaplains, Marketplace Institute at Regent College, National Faith & Work Association, Pittsburgh Leadership Foundation, Patheos Faith and Work Channel, Talbot School of Theology, and the Theology of Work Project.

Video production was provided by the team from Lamp Post Media, and Hole in the Roof Marketing designed the summit logo.

We also acknowledge the editing work carried out by Hope McPherson (Seattle Pacific University) and Patricia Anders (Hendrickson Publishers), and the work of Paul Hendrickson and the rest of the Hendrickson team.

Introduction

Albert M. Erisman

The faith at work movement really began in the Garden of Eden. In the beginning God's assignment to Adam and Eve was the only kind of work available (until the temptation to go another direction arose). Throughout the Bible and the history of the church, God has been at work, not just in personal spirituality, family, and church life, but also in the work of farming, ranching, manufacturing, statesmanship, fishing, tent-making, finance, education, government, health care, the arts, and so on. The Christian life is 24/7, not 2/1; Jesus is Lord of *all*—not just *some*—of life.

We instinctively know these things, but somehow our work lives often escape the deep and wide discipleship imperatives of biblical faith. Over the past three or four decades, a renewed faith at work integration has broken out around the church, the marketplace, and the world.

Many of us can point to organizations in the movement that were a big help to us in starting to make the connection between Sunday faith and Monday work. For some, it came from the influence of organizations such as the Christian Business Men's Connection (CBMC), Laity Lodge, Fellowship of Christian Companies International (FCCI), or the Full Gospel Business Men's Fellowship (FGBMF). For others it has been the Coalition for Christian Outreach and its Jubilee Conference, the InterVarsity Christian Fellowship (IVCF) Marketplace and Business Ministry and Urbana, or the work of Cru or Lausanne. Regent College, New College Berkeley, and LeTourneau University were *founded* with this connection as their central focus.

Individuals—including Harry Blamires, Francis Schaeffer, John Stott, Dorothy Sayers, Al Greene, Arthur Holmes, Os Guinness, and others—also contributed through their writing and speaking.

These authors approached this topic by way of worldview and a full-orbed renewal of the Christian mind. Recent Christian business leaders such as Bill Pollard, John Beckett, Cheryl Broetje, Don Flow, and Max De Pree sought to build their faith into the guiding principles of their companies. And this is just a partial list of the recent roots of the faith at work movement.

In the past few years, literature on faith at work and related topics has exploded, as have educational programs at seminaries, marketplace-based fellowships and support groups, church programs, and old and new media. In all of this, we need to be reminded that this recent work is a resurgence of what was understood and taught in various forms by the Reformers—Luther, Calvin, Wesley, and others—but seemed to have been lost. And the Theology of Work Project has shown us that this topic has always been deeply rooted in Scripture by unearthing the mountain of passages that speak directly or indirectly to the workplace.

It is clear no one person or organization has been in charge of this recent revival. Sometimes it seems that only the Holy Spirit has guided this awakening. In 2005, I encountered a group of marketplace people in Sao Paulo, Brazil. They could not point to an individual or church that started them on this pursuit, but they began gathering in homes to ask the question: What does my faith have to do with my daily work? I also met with a group of professors from various universities and various disciplines in Hong Kong. They were asking the same questions, again without prompting from a church or parachurch organization. I found a marketplace group in Delhi, India, addressing these questions, and most likely there are many other gatherings of marketplace Christians around the world. This is clearly the work of God.

The purpose of the 2014 Faith@Work Summit was to pause and address the foundational questions: Where are we now, and what is left to be done? What we found is that these easily stated questions are much more complex than they appear, primarily because there are so many lenses through which they can be analyzed.

We start by asking the question: What do we mean by connecting work and faith? We also ask: Why is this important and what is our authority for connecting faith and daily work? Then we consider the different fields of work and how both the type and position in that work can affect the way the connection between faith and work is realized. We also consider the different institutions that influence this connection from the theological foundations in the seminaries to the pastors in the churches to the preparation of workplace people in many contexts. Within these, we can ask how different ecclesiastical traditions view the connections between faith and work. While this topic could be explored beyond the Christian faith, we chose to focus on the broad topic of Christian faith and work. Finally, there are forces at work in our world—including technology, globalization, and economics—that require us to think carefully about the connection between our faith and our work in this ever-changing world in which our work is carried out.

Before we discuss the particular talks from the summit, we need to flesh out the areas that frame the different perspectives on faith and work. We will see that the framework is vast, and the summit presentations represent a small but significant sample of the big picture of what God is doing.

What Does It Mean to Connect Faith and Work?

Almost all Christians have an answer to the question: What does it mean to connect faith and work? The difficulty is that the answers look quite different depending on who you ask. I find it helpful to consider seven quite different categories many Christians have considered when they connect faith and work.[1] While

---

[1]In his book *God at Work: The History and Promise of the Faith at Work Movement*, David Miller identifies four ways people often look at what it means to connect faith and work. He uses four "E"s: Ethics,

some Christians see the connection through only one or two of
these lenses, Scripture clearly supports all seven, with no priority
order suggested by the numbering. Here is our list and a brief
explanation for each:

1. **Evangelism**. Many of those with whom we work will
   never go to church. But our being the presence of Christ
   in our world includes sharing faith with those who need
   to know Christ. How we do this requires care, because
   we are being paid by our employer to work, not to preach.
   But there are wonderful ways to do this even in the most
   hostile environments.

2. **Representation**. This deals with how we live our lives
   at work before God and before others. Far too often, our
   actions drown out our words unless the two are consistent.
   What does it look like to live out the life of Christ before
   others? Ethics is an important part of this category at
   personal, organizational, professional, and societal levels. This is not just the ethics of compliance, or the ethics of avoiding bad behavior; this is the ethics of doing
   good, which we call the ethics of mission control. Beyond
   ethics, this category also includes treating others in the
   workplace with dignity and respect—whether colleagues,
   customers, bosses, or others. In addition, Christians have
   the opportunity to demonstrate the fruit of the Spirit and
   the values of Jesus, bringing joy and hope in challenging
   situations. And, of course, it includes faithfully doing
   high-quality work.

Experience (calling and vocation, meaning of the work itself), Evangelism,
and Enrichment (developing character and spiritual practices). This is
another helpful perspective on the topic. His talk from the summit develops his approach. Darrell Cosden, in his book *A Theology of Work*, uses
a three-part description of the meaning of work: Instrumental (useful
for something other than the work), Relational (how I relate to others
through my work), and Ontological (the intrinsic value of the work itself).

3. **Service**. We work in service to others. Jesus calls us to "love our neighbors as ourselves." Paul writes to the Philippians, "in humility regard others as better than yourselves. Let each of you look not to your own interests, but to the interests of others." Every aspect of our work, from internal and external relationships to the effect of our products and services on others, deals with treating others as image-bearers of God, with dignity and respect.

4. **Meaning**. This category deals with bringing meaning and purpose to the work itself. Is the work we do of intrinsic value to the kingdom of God, or is it only a means to some other end? The first two chapters of Genesis form the basic foundation for our work in the world, and make it clear that God has invited us into his work of developing and shaping his world. Bringing meaning into our work and understanding the importance of the work itself is a vital part of connecting work and faith. We work as stewards—caretakers and developers—of a creation that belongs to God. God has designed and gifted people differently in order to play a variety of roles doing his work, as illustrated by the body of Christ. These different gifts can be used by God in diverse areas of work. Finally, if God has called us to do this work, then there is eternal value to the work of our hands, and we can expect to find continuing work in eternity.

5. **Economics**. What are the economics that come from our work—for ourselves and others? The Bible has a great deal to say about our economic mandate to create goods and services. First, we work to provide for ourselves and our households. Second, we work to generate a surplus that can be shared with others, especially those in need. Generosity should characterize the Christian at work. Third, we may have the opportunity to develop businesses that create employment for those in need of work, and in this way respond to God's call to care for the poor. We should

also recognize the problem of focusing solely on the economic return from our work (that is, working only for money), as this focus impacts us and those around us.

6. **Character development**. This category recognizes that through our work we are shaped by God and grow spiritually. Sometimes our work is just hard. Difficult work environments, tasks, and relationships, and unfair evaluations can make work painful. And sometimes success at work can create pride equally devastating to our character. Through these times God's grace can be demonstrated to others through our actions. Many people in the world have little choice about the work they do—and often have difficulty finding work. This, too, shapes us spiritually.

7. **Integration**. This deals with work as a part of a whole life, not as the only thing we do. As Christians, we see the importance of our work, but there remains a danger of focusing on our work and missing out on other aspects of life, including our families, leisure, health, corporate worship experiences, and time alone. Work and Sabbath are intimately connected in the fourth commandment. Some talk of work/life balance, but this is wrong on two counts: Work is a part of life, not a separate category, and balance will not be achieved in a fallen world. But whole-life integration can call to attention the need to make choices between needed work, rest, time with family, and so many other things.

While these seven categories represent different aspects of connecting faith and work, they work together. We need them all. For example, an unethical person at work (2) who is not generous (5), cares little about others (3), and who works all the time and does not care about his family (7) would not be the best person to share his faith (1). Similarly, it is hard to bring hope in challenging situations to others (2) if you do not believe the work that you do is meaningful (4). Growing through the challenges (6) is also visible to others (3) and is supportive of evangelism (1). One other danger: We might be tempted to prioritize these categories, making one more important than another. This is a trap. God has called us in all of these areas.

Why Is This Important?

Perhaps the primary reason Christians regard the connection between faith and work as fundamental is that it is foundational in Scripture. Far from being confined to isolated passages, the connection between faith and work runs throughout Scripture, as the Theology of Work Project has clearly shown. In addition to this, Scripture is filled with the teaching that knowing and doing are intimately connected. To know something intellectually is not enough. This faith-work connection is vital to the life of Christians in their workplaces, churches, and communities. Some fear that a focus on daily work might dilute a focus on evangelism, a mandate for all of us. Yet it is in the workplace where Christians most often encounter those who do not know God. Colleagues can see in stark relief the difference faith makes in a Christian's life. Bringing faith to work in a decidedly secular, sometimes hostile workplace requires wisdom, and begins with the quality and purpose of our work rather than our words. Further, if God has called us to this work, then we should not treat it solely as a means to some other end.

Culture

Another important perspective comes from the country or culture. Work and faith looks different in Croatia than it does in France or in the Central African Republic. It also looks different in New York City, San Francisco, or Hong Kong. Environmental context matters as well. A person from the inner city sees work (or lack of work) from yet another perspective. Rural work has a different set of demands than urban work. Cultural contexts are of vital importance in working out the how and the what of connecting faith and work.

Equippers

Two groups are, to varying degrees, supportive of Christians in the workplace. Over the past few decades, many marketplace ministry organizations emerged to come alongside Christians in the workplace—some are local, some national, and some international in their scope. In addition, there are ministries that help students link their faith and their work. In the final analysis, however, most parachurch organizations have limited reach compared with the vast number of Christians in the workplace. That makes bringing this movement into the church also vital. Both urban and suburban churches have begun to make this connection for their congregations.

Types of Work

We can look at the questions of connecting work and faith in general, but the details do matter. The vocational context in which the work is done raises additional questions. We see this across different institutions and industries. While being Christ-followers in government, business, health care, education, law, or the arts have much in common, each has its own unique opportunities and challenges. Questions of patient privacy and end-of-life issues are worked out in the context of health care; just laws and regulations are worked out in the context of law and government; and appropriate profit, the challenges of automation, and fair wages are worked out in business. All of these questions, and so many more, require contextual care, informed insight, and nuanced application for Christians of a particular profession.

Within these categories, there are more specifics to consider. Business as a broad category includes many types of enterprise: consulting, manufacturing, high tech, and agriculture, to name a few. Jobs within business include many types of works: administration, finance, marketing, engineering, manufacturing, and management. Education at a university is different from education at a seminary or in a K-12 classroom. In addition, different subjects—such as mathematics and literature—require different approaches. Each type has its own set of questions for Christians seeking to do their work to the glory of God.

The positions held in a workplace environment shape the kind of questions they raise and the opportunities and responsibilities to do something about them. An owner sees issues differently from a manager. Factory workers in a manufacturing business may not see their role in business at all, but simply as defined by the work done—a machinist, a welder, a maintenance worker. Someone without work may see work as a dream rather than a reality. A professor has a different perspective on the university than a president, dean, or food service worker. An entrepreneur seeking to build a new business has a vastly different perspective from a college librarian.

Theological Lenses

Each Christian tradition provides a perspective on work that can be useful to all. In general, there are no sharp lines between these various perspectives, or uniformity within denominational lines, but these high-level points suggest some denominational differences.[2]

---

[2] Douglas M. Strong, dean of the School of Theology and Seattle Pacific Seminary at Seattle Pacific University, provided input on this way to position different theological perspectives related to work. Alistair Mackenzie (Theology of Work Project) contributed comments and specifically

Catholics, for example, by their stress on the incremental growth of one's soul through sacramental participation, tend to speak about work through the lens of virtue formation, offering insight on issues of social justice and care for the poor.

Protestants have traditionally expected their people to be more personally engaged with the Scriptures, and differing views on work and faith have come from differing emphases on particular parts of Scripture.

Those denominations arising from the sixteenth-century Reformation—such as Lutherans, Presbyterians, and the Christian Reformed—place particular focus on God's sovereignty over all that God has made, as articulated in four themes derived from Scripture: Creation, Fall, Redemption, and Consummation. They focus on the importance of the Cultural Mandate (Genesis 1:27–28) and God's directive to join him in completing the work begun at creation.

The Anglican—and, derivatively, the Wesleyan—traditions hold to these above Reformation themes but also place particular focus on God's will to sanctify believers. Such sanctification, achieved by God's empowerment, should result in acts of piety, compassion, and justice that lead toward the new creation—all of which affect one's work.

Pentecostal denominations (such as the Assemblies of God) further this focus on God's power by emphasizing people's moment-by-moment response to the actions of the Holy Spirit, which offers insight when applied to our work.

African Americans and Christians from other nonmajority cultures often place particular focus on community identity and social context, resulting in a stress on the imperative for racial jus-

---

suggested the service category as a separate entity. Jennifer Woodruff Tait (Theology of Work Project) also provided some helpful comments on this section.

tice, economic development, and job creation. They often have a more holistic approach, with much to teach other traditions, since they were excluded from social and political institutional power.

By contrast, some more fundamentalist denominations, while they keep a praiseworthy emphasis on biblical authority, emphasize a separation from the world, with a focus on keeping oneself unspotted by worldly influences, including at one's work.

Another set of viewpoints comes from evangelical versus liberal views within denominations. Here we mean evangelical and liberal from a theological perspective rather than political, and even these lines have become confused. It is often the case that evangelicals from different denominations have more in common than either has with others in their respective denominations.

Forces on Work

The world of the twenty-first century is continuously challenged by great changes. Technology is a major contributor to these changes, disrupting individuals, societies, businesses, and other institutions. It has created a fabric of connectedness in the world known as globalization. In turn, globalization ties economic systems together in ways that impact everyone. All of these forces give rise to new types of work, new ethical issues, and new forms of joblessness.

Why These Differences Matter

The big message that your work matters to God[3] is important for any worker, paid or unpaid, in any role, and from any theological

---

[3] Doug Sherman and Bill Hendricks published a book by this title in 1987, which was the start of the conversation about connecting work and faith for many.

perspective. This is foundational. But moving beyond this broad statement, the different perspectives emerge as important. How the Catholic business owner in the United States understands the implications of "why work matters to God" looks very different from the Pentecostal factory worker, the Anglican college professor in Singapore, or the Baptist out of work in the inner city. If we are going to communicate the important message about the faith-work connection, then we must become more specific. Further, the way of thinking about the questions in the twenty-first century of technology, globalization, and economic focus will look very different from the way an eighteenth-century family farmer saw his work. A second grade teacher will face challenges and gain insights about work that look different from a city council member.

Using This Study Guide

Talks at the summit explored some of the myriad of topics raised by the many perspectives on faith and work outlined above. None of the talks represent the final word on a subject, but are designed to provoke thoughtful discussion. In this study guide, we provide an introduction to each of the talks at the 2014 Faith@Work Summit in Boston, which includes a background on the speaker, a link to the video presentation, some questions to consider in discussing the presentation, and references for further study.

We encourage you to pick a few of the presentations to start. Watch the videos, discuss the questions, and—for the curious—examine the resource list for more background. After doing a few of these, try one outside your area of interest. If you find your theological or cultural perspective is different from the presenter, then ask what other questions or issues might be relevant. This can be done as an individual, but is better in a small-group setting.

We have already noted that far more perspectives on connecting faith and work exist than are possible to represent. You can therefore approach this study guide in two ways:

- First, if a particular theological lens, cultural background, job position, or industry is not represented by one of the speakers, readers could delve into some of the foundational sections, looking for broad application to their own issues.

- A second way would be better, however. Even a scientist in a pharmaceutical lab could benefit from examining the issues of connecting work and faith in the seminary. That person could become familiar with a broader universe but then ask this important question: In what way might some of the issues from that area allow me to raise new questions in my own? In what way might the speaker's theological lens provide insight for a different lens? We believe that the care and insight raised by the various speakers for one context can be extremely helpful to someone in another context. We encourage you to take this second approach.

For the discussion of the pioneer tributes, consider a slightly different approach. The pioneers accomplished their work in a particular context of work and time, and the application discussion now looks slightly different. Ask: What could I learn from what they did to apply it to my time and context? What am I doing to provide a foundation for the next generation interested in connecting faith and work?

Finally, we have included a workplace litany, creating a commitment you can pray before God, either alone or with colleagues. For those from more formal, liturgical traditions, this will be a familiar process. Others may find it helpful as well. May God bless you as you engage with this important topic of faith and work.

Part 1: Foundations of Faith and Work

We begin with the question: Why is the connection between our faith and our work so important?

- **Katherine Leary Alsdorf** makes the case that this connection is vital for the Christian in the workplace. Beyond the individual, however, she shows it is vital to the church and to the world.

- **Will Messenger** addresses the fundamental question: Is there a biblical case for connecting faith and work? He shows that the case is not built from a few isolated Scriptures, but is a serious discussion in the whole Bible.

- **Bill Peel** challenges us to see the workplace as the most strategic mission field in the world. While some Christians are overly pushy with their faith, most don't recognize the positive impact they can have on their coworkers, colleagues, and clients through competent work, godly character, sincere concern, and wise communication. Sharing the gospel in a secular workplace can be done.

- **David Miller** wrote a book on the history of the faith and work movement in 2007. Drawing on his research, David looks at both the history and the prospects of the movement, challenging us to create faith-friendly workplaces.

- **David Gill** builds the case for an ethical foundation of our work. As Christians live out their lives before a watching world, it is essential for them to embrace ethics at work—not just in avoiding bad things, but demonstrating a higher purpose and focus for work.

Why Faith@Work Is Important: The Case

Katherine Leary Alsdorf

Biography

Katherine Alsdorf (BA, Wittenberg University; MBA, Darden School, University of Virginia) founded Redeemer Presbyterian Church's Center for Faith & Work in New York City and served as executive director from 2002 to 2012. She established the Gotham Fellows program, an entrepreneurship initiative to start new gospel-centered ventures, Arts Ministries, and numerous vocation groups. She now helps churches in other cities to establish faith and work ministries. She spent twenty-five years in the high tech industry in California and New York. She is coauthor with Tim Keller of *Every Good Endeavor: Connecting Your Work to God's Work.*

Presentation Summary

More than ever before, humanity is in a crisis over work. People change jobs and careers six times or more in their lives. Robotics will threaten even professional-level vocations over the next decade. Darwinian competition trumps teamwork and human dignity. Our work—our commitment to bring God's truth, love, and human dignity to the work lives of all people—has never been so important! How can we better equip ourselves for our work, for our calling? How do we help others work in a world that is increasingly unaware of, and even hostile to, the hope of the gospel? How does the biblical story and a deep understanding of the gospel give us the resources to persevere, the winsomeness to witness, the character to be just, and the calling to make a difference?

Video Presentation: http://bit.ly/FAWS14Alsdorf

Discussion Questions

1. What changes are happening in our society that increase the need for gospel-centered workers and leaders?

2. How might we work together to better resource and empower Christian leaders and workers in their vocational callings?

3. Why do you, as a Christian in the workplace, need the connection between work and faith?

4. In what way might this connection make a difference for your church? For the world?

Resources

Crouch, Andy. *Culture Making: Recovering Our Creative Calling*. Downers Grove, IL: InterVarsity Press, 2008.

Garber, Steve. *The Fabric of Faithfulness: Weaving Together Belief and Behavior*. Downers Grove, IL: InterVarsity Press, 2007.

Keller, Timothy. *Counterfeit Gods: The Empty Promises of Money, Sex, and Power, and the Only Hope That Matters*. New York: Viking, 2009.

Keller, Timothy, with Katherine Leary Alsdorf. *Every Good Endeavor: Connecting Your Work to God's Work*. New York: Dutton Adult, 2012.

Nelson, Tom. *Work Matters: Connecting Sunday Worship to Monday Work*. Wheaton, IL: Crossway, 2011.

Wolters, Albert M. *Creation Regained: Biblical Basis for a Reformational Worldview*. Grand Rapids: Eerdmans, 2005.

The Big Picture: God's Word on Work

William Messenger

Biography

William Messenger (BS, Case Western Reserve University; MBA, Harvard University; MDiv, Boston University; DMin, Gordon-Conwell Theological Seminary) is executive editor of the Theology of Work Project Inc., an international organization dedicated to researching, writing, and circulating materials about how the Christian faith can contribute to nonchurch workplaces. He was the director of the Mockler Center for Faith & Ethics in the Workplace at Gordon-Conwell Theological Seminary from 1999 to 2008.

Presentation Summary

Our work matters to God—but can the Bible help us in practical ways? Over the past seven years, 138 scholars, pastors, and workplace Christians from sixteen countries have researched every book of the Bible, recognizing over 1,000 passages related or directly applicable to work (www.theologyofwork.org). The Bible develops workplace applications at length, including calling, truth and deception, finance, wealth and provision, witness to Christ, relationships at work, leadership, what churches can do to equip their members to follow Christ at work, and how to make sense of suffering and hardship at work. Some applications are surprisingly specific—such as the importance of face-to-face communication in times of stress, or Jesus' process for resolving conflicts among coworkers. Others span the world of work, such as the value God places on excellence in so-called secular jobs and the preeminent role of relationships in doing good work. The Bible's ever-present message is that work is a gift from God for meeting one another's needs and making the world more as God intends it to be.

Video Presentation: http://bit.ly/FAWS14Messenger

Discussion Questions

1. What practical guidance does the Bible offer for your work and its challenges?

2. Does the Bible offer guidance for work to groups and organizations as well as to individuals? Provide examples.

3. What new ways of seeing work in Scripture discussed in this talk were helpful to you?

4. Have you had experiences in your own work life where you wished you were better equipped with biblical wisdom? What might you do now to prepare for the future?

Resources

Cosden, Darrell. *The Heavenly Good of Earthly Work*. Grand Rapids: Baker Academic, 2006.

Faith and Work Channel. http://www.Patheos.com/Faith-and-Work.

The High Calling. http://www.TheHighCalling.org.

Keller, Timothy, with Katherine Leary Alsdorf. *Every Good Endeavor: Connecting Your Work to God's Work*. New York: Dutton Adult, 2012.

Messenger, William, ed. *Theology of Work Bible Commentary*. Peabody, MA: Hendrickson, 2016.

Stevens, R. Paul. *Work Matters: Lessons from Scripture*. Grand Rapids: Eerdmans, 2012.

Theology of Work Project. http://www.TheologyofWork.org.

Witherington III, Ben. *Work: A Kingdom Perspective on Labor*. Grand Rapids: Eerdmans, 2011.

Workplace Evangelism: Appropriate Faith Conversations at Work

Bill Peel

Biography

Bill Peel (BA, Southern Methodist University; ThM, Dallas Theological Seminary; DMin, Gordon-Conwell Theological Seminary) is the founding executive director of the Center for Faith & Work at LeTourneau University (www.centerforfaithandwork.com). For more than thirty years, Bill has coached thousands of men and women to discover their calling, understand their work's significance to God, and become spiritually influential in their workplace. He is an award-winning author of seven books (available in multiple languages), including *Workplace Grace* and *What God Does When Men Pray*.

Presentation Summary

While tens of thousands are coming to Christ daily in Asia, Africa, and Latin America, the number of Christ followers in the West is in notable decline. A key reason for this decline is confusion about how closely the soul of business is tied to the business of the soul. As a result, we have followed a flawed mission strategy and neglected our most strategic mission field: the workplace. But where does evangelism fit in the workplace? Is there an important connection between godly work and faith conversations?

Video Presentation: http://bit.ly/FAWS14Peel

Discussion Questions

1. What happens when the Great Commission is disconnected from the cultural mandate?

2. Is it possible to work "as unto the Lord" without also "making the most of every opportunity" by intentionally lacing our speech with grace?

3. What does being "salt and light" in the workplace look like?

4. Have you ever shared your faith with a coworker? How did you do it and what was the reaction? Is there anything you learned from Bill that would be helpful for the next opportunity?

5. Have you seen examples of colleagues who shared their faith inappropriately at work? What did you learn from this?

Resources

Boland, John W. *Workplace Evangelism*. Mustang, OK: Tate Publishing, 2013.

Keller, Timothy. *The Reason for God: Belief in an Age of Skepticism*. New York: Dutton Adult, 2008.

Peel, Bill, and Walt Larimore. *Grace Prescriptions*. Bristol, TN: Christian Medical & Dental Associations, 2014.

———. *Workplace Grace: Becoming a Spiritual Influence in the Workplace*. Longview, TX: LeTourneau University Press, 2014.

Simpson, Michael L. *Permission Evangelism: When to Talk, When to Walk*. Colorado Springs: Cook Communications, 2003.

Charles Dickens and the Faith at Work Movement: Learning from History, Leaning into the Future

David W. Miller

Biography

David W. Miller (BA, Bucknell University; MDiv, PhD, Princeton Theological Seminary) is director of the Princeton University Faith & Work Initiative, lecturer in the Department of Religion, and president of The Avodah Institute. His research, teaching, and writing focus on the intersection of faith and work. He teaches business ethics, drawing on the resources of the Abrahamic traditions. He is the author of *God at Work: The History and Promise of the Faith at Work Movement*. David brings an unusual bilingual perspective to his scholarship. Before studying for his doctorate, he spent sixteen years in business, including eight years with IBM, and eight years in London as a senior executive in international finance. David also serves as an advisor to CEOs and executives on ethics, values, leadership, and faith at work.

Presentation Summary

In 1863, Charles Dickens published *A Christmas Carol*, in which Ebenezer Scrooge is visited by Jacob Marley and the ghosts of Christmas Past, Present, and Yet to Come. Many interpret it as a morality tale critiquing the dark side of industrialization, raising questions about the gap between rich and poor, working conditions, generosity, and even medical care.

In 2014, we still find Dickens's questions relevant. His "past, present, future" lens remains a powerful way to assess the faith at work movement. We know its past, and you've heard at this conference about the present. But where is it going, and what issues will it be responding to? Is Faith@Work just a fad that will soon run its course? Or is it a bona fide movement with staying power and the potential to impact the marketplace and its actors? To what new issues will it need to respond? Is it just a thin religious version of pop psychology designed to dampen our guilt, justify our successes and excesses, heal our failures, and fill our sense of emptiness and purposelessness at work? Or is there something theologically significant about work, our places of work, and the wider marketplace? And is there something distinctive and robust about the faith at work movement that has the potential to shape and inform attitudes toward and engagement in daily work, organizational life, and the marketplace at large?

Video Presentation: http://bit.ly/FAWS14Miller

Discussion Questions

1. How do you personally integrate your Christian faith at work?

2. How might your involvement in the faith at work movement shape and inform the nature and culture of the company you work in or lead?

3. What do you see as the challenges and possibilities of the faith at work movement in an increasingly religiously diverse workplace and global economy?

4. What was your own history of awakening to the importance of integrating your faith and work? What were important events, mentors, authors, and other influences in your personal faith at work history?

Resources

Hopper, Kenneth, and William Hopper. *The Puritan Gift: Triumph, Collapse and Revival of an American* Dream. New York: Palgrave Macmillan, 2007.

Kraemer, Hendrik. *A Theology of the Laity.* Louisville, KY: Westminster Press, 1958.

Miller, David W. *God at Work: The History and Promise of the Faith at Work Movement.* Oxford: Oxford University Press, 2006.

Mitroff, Ian, and Elizabeth Denton. *A Spiritual Audit of Corporate America: A Hard Look at Spirituality, Religion, and Values in the Workplace.* New York: Wiley & Sons, 1999.

Wuthnow, Robert. *America and the Challenges of Religious Diversity.* Princeton: Princeton University Press, 2005.

Workplace Ethics: From Damage Control to Mission Control

David W. Gill

Biography

David W. Gill (BA, University of California-Berkeley; MA, San Francisco State; PhD, University of Southern California) is an ethics writer (www.davidwgill.org) based in Oakland, California, who recently retired as Mockler-Phillips Professor of Workplace Theology & Business Ethics and director of the Mockler Center for Faith & Ethics in the Workplace at Gordon-Conwell Theological Seminary (2010–16). He taught at New College Berkeley (1977–90), North Park University (1992–2001), and St. Mary's College (2004–10). Ordained in the Progressive National Baptist Convention and an experienced organizational ethics consultant (www.ethixbiz.com), he is author of seven books, including *Becoming Good: Building Moral Character*, *Doing Right: Practicing Ethical Principles*, and *It's About Excellence: Building Ethically Healthy Organizations*.

Presentation Summary

Christians typically bring to the workplace a conviction that ethics matters and doing the right thing is a priority. We also typically argue that ethical standards are not relative and subjective but, at a foundational level, are absolute. This is all good, but we have not done enough to move beyond a dilemma-/quandary-oriented, reactive "damage control" ethics to a more biblical, proactive "mission-control" ethics. Many Christians add Bible verses but don't challenge the framework and process. We have not done enough to move beyond hardcore individualism to a more biblical team approach and beyond an abstract rules-orientation to a more biblical agent/character and corporate/culture approach. We fail to get to the missional heart of the matter. Biblical Christians are uniquely positioned to help bring a more robust mission-control ethics to the marketplaces of our world.

Video Presentation: http://bit.ly/FAWS14Gill

Discussion Questions

1. What is the nature of the ethics training and conversation at your workplace?

2. What is the mission of your organization and how does this relate to ethics? How can you, as a Christian, support the mission of your organization?

3. If you are a Christian in a largely non-Christian workplace, why would you expect to have some commonality with your colleagues even when you differ about faith?

4. How might your biblical understanding inform your discussion of ethics? How could you communicate this to your colleagues?

Resources

Beckett, John D. *Mastering Monday: A Guide to Integrating Faith & Work*. Downers Grove, IL: InterVarsity Press, 2006.

Gill, David W. "Eight Traits of an Ethically Healthy Culture: Insights from the Beatitudes." *Journal of Markets & Morality* 16, no. 2 (2013): 615–33.

———. "A Fourth Use of the Law? The Decalogue in the Marketplace. " *Journal of Religion & Business Ethics* 2, no. 2 (2011): Art. 4.

———. *It's About Excellence: Building Ethically Healthy Organizations*. Eugene, OR: Wipf & Stock, 2011.

———. "Upgrading the Ethical Decision-Making Model for Business," *Business and Professional Ethics Journal* 23, no. 4 (2004): 135–51.

MacIntyre, Alasdair. *After Virtue: A Study in Moral Theory, Second Edition*. South Bend: University of Notre Dame Press, 1984.

———. *Three Rival Versions of Moral Enquiry: Encyclopedia, Genealogy & Tradition*. South Bend: University of Notre Dame Press, 1990.

Solomon, Robert. *A Better Way to Think About Business Ethics: How Personal Integrity Leads to Corporate Success*. Oxford: Oxford University Press, 1999.

Part 2: Equipping Christians to Integrate Their Faith and Work

Taking faith with you to work needs support in many ways. Individual Bible study and prayer is vital, but so is gathering with others to learn and gain encouragement. This comes in many different flavors, as seen in the following talks.

- **Eric Welch** provides the first talk in this section on marketplace ministries. A major source of support for many Christians is the so-called marketplace ministry. These groups have been growing rapidly in recent years and are local, national, and international. They often have a particular emphasis—for example, evangelism, ethics, or accountability. They also often cater to particular audiences—for example, business leaders.

- **Mark Washington** talks about the role of campus ministries. Students, particularly at secular universities, receive an education with little connection to their faith. Campus ministries are located on many college and university sites to help fill in the gaps of a connection between their studies and their faith.

- **Paul Williams** talks about the role of the seminary in preparing pastors to lead in areas of work and faith. Seminaries represent the preparation grounds for future pastors. Thus seminaries have a role in preparing these future pastors for their role, equipping the equippers.

- **Ray Hammond** offers insight from an urban church, and **Tom Nelson** offers insight from a suburban church. Churches play *the* vital role in spiritual teaching for the whole body of Christ. Many Christians in the workplace do not have a flexible enough schedule to participate in a marketplace ministry. Often the marketplace ministry is limited in the audience it can address, and it is left to the churches to reach the rest of the people in the workplace. While the church has been criticized for ignoring the workplace where so many of its people spend so much of their time, this is changing.

Marketplace Groups: Discipleship, Fellowship, and Support

Eric Welch

Biography

Eric Welch (BS, Mississippi State University; MS, Louisiana Tech University) is vice president of Business & Sector Initiatives at the Institute for Faith, Work & Economics (www.tifwe.org), where he helps connect leaders with resources and fellowships to more fully integrate their faith with their whole lives, contributing toward a greater level of freedom, fulfillment, and flourishing in our communities. Eric's passion for this area resulted from his family, experience in the corporate world, and service in multiple lay roles in the local church. Prior to joining the institute, Eric served with Cru, where he contributed to strategic collaboration for gospel transformation and the well-being of cities. Eric also serves with Mission America Coalition/US Lausanne Committee.

Presentation Summary

A growing number of Christians are realizing the mission of God in their work through the equipping and encouragement they receive as part of marketplace and workplace ministry groups. They are serving, multiplying, and flourishing as intentional followers of Jesus right where they are, in fellowship with others. And yet the majority of Christians are still unaware of these groups! God has formed a growing infrastructure of complementary organizations to serve the gospel impact of these leaders in their family, work, community, and church. Practical content in these groups continues to deepen. God is accelerating connections between marketplace leaders in cities toward greater fruitfulness of the Great Commandment, the Great Commission, and the cultural mandate. Local faith and work networks (of multiple organizations and churches) are now forming in at least forty of the top one hundred and ten U.S. cities. Global connections are also increasing. While God is moving powerfully among these groups, there's still much work to be done!

Video Presentation: http://bit.ly/FAWS14Welch

Discussion Questions

1. How does Philippians 2:1–8 relate to our work together (as multiple organizations and churches) to help more people follow Jesus in all aspects of their lives—family, work, community, and church?

2. What marketplace groups are you familiar with in your area? How are you involved?

3. Are you being called to be a "collaborative catalyst" to help with faith and work connections and expansion in your city?

4. Why do you believe it is important to engage your city in a holistic way around the cause of the gospel? What can you envision as the impact of the gospel on your community?

Resources

Briner, Robert. *Roaring Lambs: A Gentle Plan to Radically Change Your World*. Grand Rapids: Zondervan, 1995.

Grudem, Wayne. *Business for the Glory of God: The Bible's Teaching on the Moral Goodness of Business*. Wheaton, IL: Crossway, 2003.

Guinness, Os. *The Call: Finding and Fulfilling the Central Purpose of Your Life*. Nashville: Thomas Nelson, 1998.

Hillman, Os. *Faith@Work*. Fairfield, CT: Aslan Publishing, 2004.

Hunter, James Davidson. *To Change the World: The Irony, Tragedy, and Possibility of Christianity in the Late Modern World*. Oxford: Oxford University Press, 2010.

Keller, Timothy, with Katherine Leary Alsdorf. *Every Good Endeavor: Connecting Your Work to God's Work*. New York: Dutton Adult, 2012.

Miller, David W. *God at Work: The History and Promise of the Faith at Work Movement*. Oxford: Oxford University Press, 2006.

Nelson, Tom. *Work Matters: Connecting Sunday Worship to Monday Work*. Wheaton, IL: Crossway, 2011.

Russell, Mark L., and Dave Gibbons. *Our Souls at Work*. London: Russell Media, 2010.

Sherman, Doug, and William Hendricks. *Your Work Matters to God*. Colorado Springs: NavPress, 1990.

Spada, Doug, and Dave Scott. *Monday Morning Atheist: Why We Switch God Off at Work and How You Fix It*. McKenny, TX: Worklife Press, 2012.

Whelchel, Hugh. *How Then Should We Work? Rediscovering the Biblical Doctrine of Work*. Wheaton, IL: WestBow, 2012.

University and Student Groups: Coming Alongside the Next Generation

Mark Washington

Biography

Mark Washington (BS, Iowa State University; MBA, North Park University; MA in Theological Studies, North Park Theological Seminary) is the national coordinator of MBA Ministry for InterVarsity Christian Fellowship/USA. For twelve years he has partnered with faculty and students to develop witnessing communities at top-tier MBA programs to transform the people, ideas, and structures of business schools. He serves on the National Faith & Work Association launching team and is the convener for the Chicagoland Workplace Ministers Network. He is ordained in the Evangelical Covenant Church.

Presentation Summary

The future of the faith and work movement will depend upon its leadership—the next generation. Millennials are eager to impact the world and are ripe for partnership and mentoring. To invest in the next generation, we should first seek to understand who they are and what they need from us. As a practical case study, mentoring provides a window into their lives and stimulates discussion about changes we need to make to help them steward their lives and influence for Christ. Suggestions and resources for mentors will be presented, as well as strategies for developing the next generation of faith and work leaders for success.

Video Presentation: http://bit.ly/FAWS14Washington

Discussion Questions

1. What might you do to invest in the next generation of believers in business?

2. What changes or next steps do you need to take in order to be a good partner or mentor to a next generation leader?

3. What has been your own experience of being mentored? Of mentoring others? Did any of this start in your college days?

4. How does Mark's insight about the next generation compare with your experience? Are there ways to both understand and challenge the next generation to live out their faith in the workplace?

Resources

Dunn, Richard R., and Jana L. Sundene. *Shaping the Journey of Emerging Adults: Life-Giving Rhythms for Spiritual Transformation.* Downers Grove, IL: InterVarsity Press, 2012.

Hyun, Jane, and Audrey S. Lee. *Flex: The New Playbook for Managing Across Differences.* New York: HarperBusiness, 2014.

Kim, David H. *20 and Something: Have the Time of Your Life (And Figure It All Out Too).* Grand Rapids: Zondervan, 2014.

Urban, Tim. "Why Generation Y Yuppies Are Unhappy." *Huffington Post* (blog). Sept. 15, 2013. http://www.huffingtonpost .com/wait-but-why/generation-y-unhappy_b_3930620.

Research on Millennials at work can be found at the following websites:

- http://www.barna.org/barna-update/millennials

- http://www.pwc.com/gx/en/hr-management-services /publications/nextgen-study.jhtml

- http://www.pewresearch.org/topics/millennials

Theological Education: Rethinking What's Important

Paul Williams

Biography

Paul Williams (BA, MA, MSc, University of Oxford; MCS, Regent College) is executive director of the Marketplace Institute and the David J. Brown Family Chair of Marketplace Theology & Leadership at Regent College (Vancouver, British Columbia). He was formerly chief economist and head of international research for DTZ, a London-based multinational consulting and investment banking group. Paul is passionate about the church's missional engagement with contemporary culture. He served as academic dean at Regent and has helped pioneer a number of innovations in theological education, including the *ReFrame* project (www.reframecourse.com) and a new executive program for marketplace leaders.

Presentation Summary

Whether through excellence, absence, or mediocrity, theological education has a huge influence on the church's devotional and missional life, and this is no less true for those seeking to live faithfully and fruitfully as disciples of Jesus Christ in the marketplace. In recent decades, a host of new programs, courses, and resources have been developed by seminaries, theological schools, and Bible colleges to help marketplace believers. How do we evaluate these? In what other ways could these educational institutions support faith at work? In addition to these questions, we need to ask some broader ones: What is the role of the local church in theological education? Are the institutions of theological education currently fit for purpose, and will their response to the current crisis in theological education help or hinder the faith

at work movement? We'll consider these questions in the context
of seeking to grasp the opportunities that our present moment
offers us—a moment in which both the need and the awareness
of the need for quality theological education for faith and work
integration are growing.

Video Presentation: http://bit.ly/FAWS14Williams

Discussion Questions

1. What are the biggest challenges facing ordinary Christians seeking to live faithfully in the workplace, and how are these challenges related to theological education?

2. Typically, where do such believers seek answers to the problems, challenges, and questions they face in living faithfully at work?

3. How could the theological resources for faith at work integration that theological institutions already have be made available in a better way to those who need them?

4. As a workplace Christian, have you considered the value of more formal theological education? Why or why not?

Resources

Ellul, Jacques. *The Presence of the Kingdom*. Colorado Springs: Helmers & Howard, 1989.

Mouw, Richard J., and Andy Crouch. "Seminary of the Future Project." Fuller Theological Seminary, 2011. http://www.future.fuller.edu.

ReFrame Project. http://www.reframecourse.com.

Rozko, J. R., and Doug Paul. "The Missiological Future of Theological Education." Unpublished paper. http://www.thefutureoftheologicaleducation.com.

Smith, David. *Mission after Christendom*. London: Darton, Longman & Todd, 2003.

Workplace Disciples in the Urban Church and Community

Ray Hammond

Biography

Ray Hammond (BA, MA, MD, Harvard University) served as a physician at Cape Cod Hospital in Hyannis, Massachusetts. He was called to the preaching ministry in 1976 and is founder and pastor of Bethel African Methodist Episcopal Church in Boston. He is the author of several papers and articles on a range of issues, including diversity and violence prevention. He is also the cofounder of the Boston TenPoint Coalition—a group of inner-city churches committed to addressing the needs of young people at high and proven risk for violence, especially in communities of color.

Presentation Summary

Faith@Work in the church, and especially in the urban church, begins with an ethic of servant-leadership. It also takes to heart the belief, echoed in Ephesians 4:12, that a critical work of the church is to equip Jesus' people for "works of service," and a significant part of that service must happen in the workplace. From that vantage point, it wrestles with a host of questions: How can the church be a force for good in helping motivate, shape, and encourage its members to take their faith and values to work in redemptive ways? How can church life itself be a model and train young people for workplace success? How can the church contribute to educational opportunity, job creation, entrepreneurship, and community economic development so there actually is some opportunity for work in order to integrate one's faith?

Video Presentation: http://bit.ly/FAWS14RHammond

Discussion Questions

1. How do the church and its members see the workplace not just as a source of income or career opportunities, but also as a place to which we are called by God?

2. Alongside whatever government and corporate programs there may be for job creation and training, what could your church do as God's "third force" in the economy?

3. How might our churches best counter the ethics and values of today's streets and the entertainment media with an attractive, compelling Christian alternative that includes a positive vision of work and business?

4. What key insights did you take away from Ray's talk? In what ways could you apply Ray's ideas in your own world?

Resources

Flake, Floyd, and Donna Marie Williams. *The Way of the Boot-strapper: Nine Action Steps for Achieving Your Dreams.* New York: Amistad, 2000.

Larive, Armand E. *After Sunday: A Theology of Work.* London: Bloomsbury Academic, 2004.

Shannahan, Chris. *Voices from the Borderland: Re-Imagining Cross-Cultural Urban Theology in the Twenty-First Century.* London: Equinox, 2010.

Walls, Julius Jr., and Kevin Lynch. *Mission, Inc. The Practitioner's Guide to Social Enterprise.* Oakland, CA: Berrett-Koehler Publications, 2009.

Faith@Work in the Suburban Church: Neighborly Love—Why Both Compassion and Capacity Matter

Tom Nelson

Biography

Tom Nelson (ThM, Dallas Theological Seminary; DMin, Trinity Evangelical Divinity School) has been senior pastor of Christ Community Church in Leawood, Kansas, for more than twenty years. He is the author of *Five Smooth Stones: Discovering the Path to Wholeness of Soul* and *Ekklesia: Rediscovering God's Design for the Church*. His newest book is *Work Matters: Connecting Sunday Worship to Monday Work*. He serves on the boards of The Gospel Coalition and Trinity International University.

Presentation Summary

With all the multifaceted challenges of the modern-day global economy, one of the most compelling cries of the contemporary world is for jobs. How is the church responding to this cry? Are we missing something? A closer examination of Jesus' teaching on the Great Commandment, particularly as our Lord illustrates its revolutionary message with the story of the Good Samaritan, helps apprentices of Jesus better connect Sunday faith with Monday work. In his story of the Good Samaritan, Jesus teaches that neighborly love requires not only heartfelt compassion but also economic capacity. If we are going to take Jesus' teaching seriously, then we not only need to teach a robust theology that informs people's work and collaborative economic life; we must also become redemptive communities where diligent work is encouraged and economic wisdom is taught, indwelled, and celebrated.

Video Presentation: http://bit.ly/FAWS14Nelson

Discussion Questions

1. Why is it important to understand the real needs of employment and culture in our own communities? What does this have to do with the gospel? How did Tom illustrate this in his talk?

2. Why is there often such a wide gap between our understanding of faith and economics? How important is that gap, and how might we begin to narrow it in our faith community?

3. How is compassion for others connected to economics? What is the importance of understanding the common good? How should economics and the common good affect our theology?

4. How might we enhance our economic capacity so that we can more faithfully, wisely, and generously serve the poor, the unemployed, the marginalized, and the under-resourced?

Resources

Brown, Peter. *Through the Eye of a Needle: Wealth, the Fall of Rome, and the Making of Christianity in the West, 350–550 AD*. Princeton: Princeton University Press, 2014.

Garber, Steve. *Visions of Vocation: Common Grace for the Common Good*. Downers Grove, IL: InterVarsity Press, 2014.

Grudem, Wayne, and Barry Asmus. *The Poverty of Nations: A Sustainable Solution*. Wheaton, IL: Crossway, 2013.

Gwartney, James D., Richard L. Stroup, Dwight R. Lee, and Tawni Hunt Ferrarini. *Common Sense Economics: What Everyone Should Know About Wealth and Prosperity*. New York: St. Martin's Press, 2010.

Nelson, Tom. *Work Matters: Connecting Sunday Worship to Monday Work*. Wheaton, IL: Crossway, 2011.

Schneider, John R. *The Good of Affluence: Seeking God in a Culture of Wealth*. Grand Rapids: Eerdmans, 2002.

Sherman, Amy L. *Kingdom Calling: Vocational Stewardship for the Common Good*. Downers Grove, IL: InterVarsity Press, 2011.

Sowell, Thomas. *Basic Economics: A Common Sense Guide to the Economy*. New York: Basic Books, 2007.

Part 3: Perspectives from Different Workplaces

In the introduction we argued that integrating faith and work looks a bit different depending on the type of work being done, the type of organization, the position within the organization, and many other factors. At the summit, we brought multiple perspectives on work seen through the eyes of those in the workplace. There are a diverse set of questions here including:

1. How do I do my work as a Christian?

2. Can I influence the product of the work to better reflect kingdom values?

3. Can I influence the structure of the workplace to better reflect kingdom values?

- **Gloria Nelund** worked at the executive level at Deutsche-bank, the only woman at that level. She went on to found Tri-Link Global, an investment company developing businesses in many parts of the world. Her story gives insight on gender roles and relationships at work, and what it means to lead at senior levels.

- **Bill Pollard** was the CEO and chairman of the global ServiceMaster Company. He provided leadership to people from different cultures and responsibilities around the world. As a Christian at a publicly traded company, he established as the first value of that company "To honor God in all we do." His story provides insight for top-level leadership.

- **Cheryl Broetje**, with her husband Ralph, started Broetje Orchards with humble beginnings, but which now has five million trees and sells apples around the world. Their labor force shifted over the years, and they have worked at shaping a workplace culture. They developed a strategy of empowerment for their people that changes lives, as well as delivering fruit to the world.

- **Larry Ward** works as a bi-vocational pastor in the inner city of Boston. Creating jobs for people looking for work became a passion for him, and he began an entrepreneurship program through his church. He talks about training for entrepreneurship, launching businesses, and developing hope in the name of Christ.

- **Albert Erisman** speaks about the work of education. Colleges and universities face substantial challenges as their work is under significant pressure. For the Christian at the academy, the challenges include understanding and developing a Christian perspective on their subject matter, going beyond the transfer of knowledge to shape character in the future generations, and doing this in an affordable manner.

Salting a Corporation: Faithful Impact in a Larger Organization

Gloria Nelund

Biography

Gloria Nelund spent nearly thirty years on Wall Street as one of the most successful executives in the international investment management industry. After retiring from Deutsche Bank, she co-founded TriLinc Global, an investment firm dedicated to creating investment products that attract significant private capital to help solve some of the world's most pressing issues. In 2013, TriLinc launched a $1.25 billion impact fund for U.S. retail investors to provide growing businesses in select developing economies. Gloria is also chair and independent trustee for RS Investments' $22 billion mutual fund complex, as well as a frequent guest lecturer at several top business schools.

Presentation Summary

While Gloria lived by a personal commitment to honor God in all she did on Wall Street, she felt guilty about having a career in business—especially one she enjoyed that brought her significant personal rewards. In 2005, she retired to finally "serve God," and after an almost three-year "wilderness" journey of desperately seeking her purpose, God demonstrated that her job had been her mission field. In this video, she highlights her journey, disclosing her three "secrets to success" (working hard, solving problems, and helping people) in navigating a career in some of the largest organizations in the world, offering some insight about being the only woman in the male-dominated investment industry, and revealing the one book that influenced all of her actions and perspectives.

Video Presentation: http://bit.ly/FAWS14Nelund

Discussion Questions

1. How aware are you that our actions may speak so loudly that no one can hear what we're saying?

2. Do you pay attention to where God is already working in your life, and do you make yourself available to join him in his work?

3. Gloria thought she needed to leave her "secular job" to serve God full time, yet she learned something else about her work. What can you learn from her story?

4. How did Gloria deal with gender issues at work? In what ways did she model a work ethic?

Resources

Blackaby, Henry T. *Experiencing God: Knowing and Doing the Will of God*. Nashville: B&H Books, 2008.

Buford, Bob. *Drucker and Me: What a Texas Entrepreneur Learned from the Father of Modern Management*. Franklin, TN: Worthy Publishing, 2007.

Eldred, Ken, and David Yonggi Cho. *God Is at Work: Transforming People and Nations through Business*. New York: Regal Books, 2009.

Jones, Laurie Beth. *Jesus, CEO: Using Ancient Wisdom for Visionary Leadership*. New York: Hachette Books, 1996.

Messenger, William, ed. *Theology of Work Bible Commentary*. Peabody, MA: Hendrickson, 2016.

Pollard, C. William. *Serving Two Masters? Reflections on God and Profit*. New York: HarperCollins, 2006.

Silvoso, Ed. *Anointed for Business: How to Use Your Influence in the Marketplace to Change the World*. New York: Regal Books, 2006.

Traeger, Sebastian, and Greg D. Gilbert. *The Gospel at Work: How Working for King Jesus Gives Purpose and Meaning to Our Jobs*. Grand Rapids: Zondervan, 2014.

Ziglar, Zig. *Better Than Good: Creating a Life You Can't Wait to Live*. Nashville: Thomas Nelson, 2007.

The Soul of the Faith@Work Movement

Bill Pollard

Biography

Bill Pollard (BA, Wheaton College; JD, Northwestern University School of Law) serves as chair of Fairwyn Investment Co., a private investment firm. For twenty-five years he participated in the leadership of The ServiceMaster Company, serving not once but twice as its CEO. During Bill's leadership, ServiceMaster was recognized as the #1 service company among the Fortune 500. He has served as a director of a number of public companies and charitable and religious organizations, including Wheaton College and The Billy Graham Evangelistic Association. He is the author of several books including the best-selling *The Soul of the Firm*. His most recent book is *The Tides of Life*. He has been recognized by leading business schools, including Harvard and Notre Dame, for his business ethics and leadership in the development of people.

Presentation Summary

The world that God so loves includes the people we work with and serve. Each one has been created in the image and likeness of God, with their own fingerprint of potential and a soul that will live beyond this life. They represent the only thing that has eternal value in our work. They are the soul of the Faith@Work Movement. We are called to be ambassadors of Christ in our work with God making his appeal through us. Our work provides a unique opportunity not only to excel in what we do but also to live and share our faith. In so doing, we learn how to love and worship God on the horizontal as we engage the people with whom we work and serve.

Video Presentation: http://bit.ly/FAWS14Pollard

Discussion Questions

1. Where is the church today and where should it be tomorrow in teaching and supporting our work, whatever it may be, as a ministry and a high calling of God?

2. What does it mean to be an ambassador for Christ in the marketplace? What does servant-leadership look like?

3. How should we view those in our workplaces who are not Christ-followers? How did Bill's company connect "Honor God in all that we do" with caring for a diverse workforce?

4. How did the ideas of caring for people and making a profit fit together? Does God's calling include making a profit?

Resources

Carey, George, and Andrew Carey. *We Don't Do God: The Marginalization of Public Faith.* Oxford: Monarch Books, 2012.

Eldred, Ken. *God Is at Work: Transforming People and Nations Through Business.* Grand Rapids: Regal Books, 2005.

Keller, Timothy. *The Reason for God: Belief in an Age of Skepticism.* New York: Viking, 2008.

Laity Lodge Leadership Forum. "Faith in the Workplace: Presentations from the 1999 Laity Lodge Leadership Forum, Sea Island, GA." http://104.131.17.164/keyword/faith-in-the-workplace -presentations-from-the-1999-laity-lodge-leadership-forum -sea-island-georgia.pdf.

Miller, David W. *God at Work: The History and Promise of the Faith at Work Movement.* Oxford: Oxford University Press, 2006.

Nash, Laura, and Scotty McLennan. *Church on Sunday, Work on Monday: The Challenge of Fusing Christian Values with Business Life.* San Francisco: Jossey-Bass, 2001.

Nicholl, Armand. *The Question of God: C. S. Lewis and Sigmund Freud Debate God, Love, Sex, and the Meaning of Life.* Glencoe, IL: Free Press, 2003.

Novak, Michael. *Business as a Calling: Work and the Examined Life.* Glencoe, IL: Free Press, 2013.

Pollard, C. William. *The Soul of the Firm.* New York: Harper-Business, 2010.

———. *The Tides of Life: Learning to Lead and Serve as You Navigate the Currents of Life.* Wheaton, IL: Crossway, 2014.

Shaping Workers: Calling, Valuing, Training, and Empowering

Cheryl Broetje

Biography

Cheryl Broetje and her husband Ralph founded, own, and operate Broetje Orchards—a vertically integrated apple-growing, packing, shipping, and sales company located in the southeastern part of Washington State. Its five million trees produce fruit exported around the world, and Broetje Orchards's mission is to be "a quality fruit company bearing fruit, fruit that will last." Cheryl also founded The Center for Sharing, a nonprofit, faith-based servant-leadership development organization whose mission is "calling forth the gifts of all persons through Christ-centered community"; she continues to serve as its executive director. Her passion is in bringing people and resources together to build kingdom structures.

Presentation Summary

Ralph Broetje had a daydream when he was fifteen years old to one day own an orchard and help kids in India. But early into his and Cheryl's farming years, their labor force radically changed from white, U.S. citizens to Latino immigrants. They realized their employees must become their first focus of mission if they were ever to help kids in India. The work provided a common focus that compelled them to show up every day and do their best. But their new employees not only needed skills; they also needed affordable housing, dependable child care, and year-round jobs if their kids were going to stay in school and flourish. Most of all, they needed to feel safe. The Broetjes find that practicing the core values of love, compassion, respect, community, and purpose helps them care about others. They take better care of their place, which in turn takes care of them, with a surplus of love to export.

Video Presentation: http://bit.ly/FAWS14Broetje

Discussion Questions

1. Do the people you serve at work feel emotionally and physically safe and welcome?

2. What are you doing to promote that kind of corporate culture? What did Cheryl do?

3. What core values are currently operating in your organization? How do they show up in your practices and policies?

4. Are people becoming healthier, wiser, freer, more likely to serve others as a result (see Robert Greenleaf's "test" for servant-leaders)? Why is that important?

Resources

Bloom, Sandra L. *Creating Sanctuary: Toward the Evolution of Sane Societies*. London: Routledge, 2013.

Evans, Alice Frazer, Robert A. Evans, and William Bean Kennedy. *Pedagogies for the Non-Poor*. Maryknoll, NY: Orbis Books, 1987.

Greenleaf, Robert. *Servant Leadership: A Journey into the Nature of Legitimate Power and Greatness*. New York: Paulist Press, 1991.

Hawken, Paul. *Blessed Unrest: How the Largest Social Movement in the World Came into Being and Why No One Saw It Coming*. London: Penguin Group, 2007.

Wheatley, Margaret J. *Finding Our Way: Leadership for an Uncertain Time*. Oakland, CA: Berrett-Koehler Publishers, 2005.

Creating Jobs: Entrepreneurship and Community Economic Development

Larry Ward

Biography

Larry Ward (BS, Northeastern University; MEd, University of Massachusetts) has been pastor of the Abundant Life Church (Cambridge, Massachusetts) for twenty years. He is a certified trainer for the National Foundation for Teaching Entrepreneurship (NFTE) and Financial Education Associates (financial literacy and homeownership). He is an entrepreneurship course instructor for the Boston campus of Gordon-Conwell Theological Seminary.

Presentation Summary

The psalmist says, "The heavens declare the glory of God; the skies proclaim the work of his hands" (Psalm 19:1 NIV). Beauty is all around us, and nature testifies to the fact that God works. God made us in his image and likeness (Genesis 1:26), and he has given us talents and abilities. Work is a primary means for each of us to express our God-given creativity. But creating jobs is not just about us and our needs. It is about serving the needs of others. As the population grows and traditional workplaces downsize, more people will be searching for meaningful work and there will be more needs for businesses to meet. Neither Washington nor Wall Street will be able to meet the challenge. Christians and churches not only can, but also must, step up to the challenge and nurture entrepreneurship and job creation.

Video Presentation: http://bit.ly/FAWS14Ward

Discussion Questions

1. What steps did Larry Ward take to address the need for jobs in his own church?

2. How does "out-of-the-box" thinking affect the way a church might engage its community?

3. How might collaborations between churches, parachurch organizations, seminaries, and foundations work together to develop and support more entrepreneurs? Could you apply some of the ideas Larry introduced to your own context?

4. In what way does the development of entrepreneurship support the kingdom of God in a community?

Resources

Goosen, Richard J., and R. Paul Stevens. *Entrepreneurial Leadership: Finding Your Calling, Making a Difference.* Downers Grove, IL: InterVarsity Press, 2013.

Guillebeau, Chris. *The $100 Start-Up: Reinvent the Way You Make a Living, Do What You Love, and Create a New Future.* New York: Crown Business, 2012.

Kawasaki, Guy. *The Art of the Start: The Time-Tested, Battle-Hardened Guide for Anyone Starting Anything.* London: Penguin/Portfolio, 2004.

Yunus, Muhammad. *Banker to the Poor: Micro-Lending and the Battle against World Poverty.* New York: PublicAffairs, 2003.

Faith at Work at the University: Rethinking What's Important

Albert M. Erisman

Biography

Albert M. Erisman (BS, Northern Illinois University; MS, PhD, Iowa State University) is executive in residence at the Seattle Pacific University School of Business, Government, and Economics. He also cochairs the Theology of Work Project (www.theologyofwork.org) and cofounded and edits *Ethix* magazine (www.ethix.org). He previously served as a senior technical fellow and director of R&D in technology and mathematics at The Boeing Company (1969–2001). He is author or editor of six books, including *Direct Methods for Sparse Matrices* with I. S. Duff and J. K. Reid (Oxford: Clarendon Press, 1989), *The Purpose of Business*, and *The Accidental Executive: Lessons on Business, Faith, and Calling from the Life of Joseph*.

Presentation Summary

Christians in the academy have a wonderful opportunity to represent the kingdom of God in their world of work and to influence the next generation. It starts with scholarship and teaching. How do we use the lens of Scripture to gain insight and understanding that can be communicated both to our Christian colleagues and in a more secular environment? Al illustrates this with research on the purpose of business carried out at Seattle Pacific University and research on leadership at Claremont University. Another area where Christians can offer insight is in helping students create a foundation of values and character. A third area he addresses calls for Christian leadership to create a response to the escalating costs of university education.

Video Presentation: http://bit.ly/FAWS14Erisman

Discussion Questions

1. What are some areas for Christian scholarship you can identify that meet a need in the world?

2. What are our key contributions around the development of character at universities?

3. Can we offer ways to break the cost curve, while dealing with character development and new ideas in curriculum?

4. Might it be possible to focus on the traditional areas of content creation, contextual understanding, and character development over a shorter, more intense period, dealing with knowledge acquisition in a more cost-effective way?

5. For those in workplaces other than education, what tensions might exist between products, relationships, and profit?

Resources

DeMillo, Richard A. *Abelard to Apple: The Fate of American Colleges and Universities*. New York: Jossey-Bass, 2011.

Erisman, Albert M. *The Accidental Executive: Lessons on Business, Faith, and Calling from the Life of Joseph*. Peabody, MA: Hendrickson, 2015.

Erisman, Albert M., and David Gautschi, eds. *The Purpose of Business: Contemporary Perspectives from Different Walks of Life*. London: Palgrave Macmillan, 2015.

Khurana, Rakesh. *From Higher Aims to Hired Hands: The Social Transformation of American Business Schools and the Unfulfilled Promise of Management as a Profession*. Princeton: Princeton University Press, 2007.

Maciarello, Joseph, and Karen Linkletter. *Drucker's Lost Art of Management: Peter Drucker's Timeless Vision for Building Effective Organizations*. New York: McGraw-Hill Education, 2011.

Selingo, Jeffrey. *College Unbound: The Future of Higher Education and What It Means for Students*. New York: Houghton-Mifflin, 2013.

Van Duzer, Jeff. *Why Business Matters to God (And What Still Needs to Be Fixed)*. Downers Grove, IL: IVP Academic, 2010.

Part 4: Forces Affecting Our Work

Major forces in the twenty-first century make work more challenging and cause us to reexamine what it means to be a Christian at work. Of course, each of these areas represents fields of work for Christians, and the following talks develop not only the impact on other work but also what it means to be a Christian in these areas.

- **John Dyer** looks at technology through a Christian lens. Technology has been a powerful force for a long time, but in recent years its impact is transforming the world of work. It creates great new opportunities, and at the same time creates disruptions that change these opportunities for work and our own personal lives.

- **Tim Liu** offers his Christian perspective on this powerful force. Globalization is a natural response to technology, making communication and transportation more broadly available. This moves the impact of our work from local to global, and affects the way we see the world and our work in that world.

- **Greg Forster** develops one Christian view of the impact of economics, and **Julius Walls** looks at this force through the lens of the poor and marginalized in society. In part because of technology and globalization, economics has moved to the center of discussion about work. Many more options are available when considering the economics of a business, and as is the case with other forces, this one creates great opportunity along with significant downsides.

Workplace Technology: Thinking Theologically about IT

John Dyer

Biography

John Dyer (BS, Texas A&M University; ThM, Dallas Theological Seminary; PhD candidate, Durham University) is executive director of Communications and Educational Technology for DTS. As a web developer, he has built tools for companies including Apple, Microsoft, Harley-Davidson, Anheuser-Busch, and the U.S. Department of Defense, and his code libraries are now used in more than 10 million websites. He also develops secure Bible software for closed countries and is the author of *From the Garden to the City: The Redeeming and Corrupting Power of Technology.*

Presentation Summary

Choosing which new technologies to implement in a business usually involves a cost/benefit analysis and a consultant whose only answer is, "Install Oracle." But is it possible to think theologically about our technology? Do those ancient Scriptures that speak of the afterlife and spiritual salvation have any guidance that goes beyond Google's own advice to "Do no evil"? In this session, we'll see that the story told in the Scriptures is deeply concerned with human making, both ancient and new. We'll also see that technology has the power to shape environments, including the workplace. Finally, Dyer concludes with some directions for thinking about technology in the workplace through the lens of Scripture.

Video Presentation: http://bit.ly/FAWS14Dyer

Discussion Questions

1. How can you use technology in a way that more deeply reflects your Creator and his purposes?

2. The effects of technology on individuals and organizations can be both positive and negative. How might Christians speak into this challenging arena?

3. What are ways that we, as Christians, can address the issues of job loss due to technology?

4. Do your current choices regarding technology reflect your own values and/or the priorities of your workplace?

5. What is the connection between technology and the Sabbath? Why should we seek to think creatively about the Sabbath in this technological age?

Resources

Brende, Eric. *Better Off: Flipping the Switch on Technology.* New York: Harper Perennial, 2004.

Dyer, John. *From the Garden to the City: The Redeeming and Corrupting Power of Technology.* Grand Rapids: Kregel Publications, 2011.

McKinsey & Company. "The social economy: Unlocking value and productivity through social technologies." July 2012. http://www.mckinsey.com/insights/high_tech_telecoms_internet/the_social_economy.

Powers, William. *Hamlet's BlackBerry: A Practical Philosophy for Building a Good Life in the Digital Age.* New York: Harper Perennial, 2011.

"Zen and the Workplace," on *Zen & Tech* (podcast). http://www.imore.com/zen-tech-58-zen-workplace.

Godly Globalization

Timothy S. Liu

Biography

Timothy S. Liu (BSEE, University of Wisconsin Madison; MBA, Arcadia University) is the business development director for Asia, a tech company in advanced control and optimization for pharmaceutical, water, nutritional, and pulp and paper processes. He serves as senior associate for Lausanne Committee for World Evangelization for Marketplace Ministry. Founder and director of Marketplace Christian Network since 2001, he is also a council member of the Biblical Graduate School of Theology in Singapore and former president of the Graduates' Christian Fellowship Singapore (2007–2014). Timothy is a resource person for the East Asia Graduates' Conference (a movement of IFES East Asia) for the marketplace. His passion is to help believers integrate faith and life.

Presentation Summary

Globalization, though not a new phenomenon in history, is causing major shifts and massive impact on social structures and identity, economy, technology, and migration. How can Christians, through Christ's cosmic redemptive plan, bring the whole gospel to the world through their daily work in business, health care, public administration, technology, urban planning, manufacturing, arts, culture, and many other areas?

Video Presentation: http://bit.ly/FAWS14Liu

Discussion Questions

1. What evidence do you see of the conflicting forces of globalization and localization? What insight do we gain on these issues through our Christian faith?

2. How do the forces of globalization affect poverty and wage disparity? Do Christians have anything to say into this growing challenge?

3. How does globalization affect the way we think about our identities?

4. What does it mean that Christ is redeeming the cosmos? How can you contribute to *shalom* in your community through your work?

5. Tim suggested we minister in our world of work. How could you apply this to your own work?

Resources

Charan, Ram. *Global Tilt: Leading Your Business through the Great Economic Power Shift*. New York: Crown Business, 2013.

Jenkins, Philip. *The Next Christendom: The Coming of Global Christianity*. Oxford: Oxford University Press, 2011.

Lee, Jean. *Two Pillars of the Market: A Paradigm for Dialogue between Theology and Economics*. New York: Lang, 2011.

Stiglitz, Joseph E. *Making Globalization Work*. New York: W. W. Norton, 2006.

Stewardship Economics: Work in the Larger Economic Frame

Greg Forster

Biography

Greg Forster is a program director in the Faith, Work, and Economics program of the Kern Family Foundation. He directs the Oikonomia Network (www.oikonomianetwork.org), a national learning community of theological educators and evangelical seminaries dedicated to helping pastors connect biblical wisdom, sound theology, and good stewardship to work and the economy. He is also the author of six books and numerous scholarly and popular articles, a senior fellow at the Friedman Foundation for Educational Choice, and a regular contributor to several online outlets. He received a doctorate with distinction in political philosophy from Yale University.

Presentation Summary

We are made for community, and work is one of the most important ways human beings relate to one another. When we work together as fellow stewards of the world, we weave the fabric of culture and civilization. Throughout history, the great champions of vocation—from Moses to Solomon, the apostle Paul to Gregory the Great, and Luther to Wesley—did not stop with the personal meaning of work. They offered a powerful witness to the public meaning of work, demanding that organizations and social systems recognize the equal dignity of all human beings, treating them all as stewards of the world. Today's entrepreneurial economy was largely built by their witness. If we want to help people love one another, do justice, flourish, and live as disciples 24/7, then we must renew this public witness in our time.

Video Presentation: http://bit.ly/FAWS14Forster

Discussion Questions

1. How are trust and stewardship combined in our economic system? What difference does that make? Have you experienced this in your own activity in the marketplace?

2. How does this stewardship concept extend to love of neighbor as Greg develops it?

3. What would it mean to develop grace-based communities through this economic system?

4. How do we extend our understanding of work to the public meaning of work? Why is this important? How does it represent the kingdom of God?

Resources

Acton Institute. *For the Life of the World: Letters to the Exiles.* Grand Rapids: Acton Institute, 2015. http://www.letterstothe exiles.com.

Bolt, John. *Economic Shalom: A Reformed Primer on Faith, Work, and Human Flourishing.* Grand Rapids: Christian Library Press, 2013.

Claar, Victor, and Robin Klay. *Economics in Christian Perspective: Theory, Policy and Life Choices.* Downers Grove, IL: IVP Academic, 2007.

Cleveland, Drew, and Greg Foster, eds. *The Pastor's Guide to Fruitful Work and Economic Wisdom: Understanding What Your People Do All Day.* Overland Park, KS: Made to Flourish, 2012.

DeKoster, Lester. *Work: The Meaning of Your Life; A Christian Perspective.* Grand Rapids: Acton Institute, 2010.

De Soto, Hernando. *The Mystery of Capital: Why Capitalism Succeeds in the West and Fails Everywhere Else.* New York: Basic Books, 2003.

Economic Wisdom Project. "A Christian Vision for Flourishing Communities." Oikonomia Network, 2013. http://oikonomia network.org.

Forster, Greg. *Theology That Works: Making Disciples Who Practice Fruitful Work and Economic Wisdom in Modern America.* Oikonomia Network, 2014. http://oikonomianetwork.org.

Greer, Peter, and Chris Horst. *Entrepreneurship for Human Flourishing.* Washington, DC: AEI Press, 2014.

Orbett, Steve, and Brian Fikkert. *When Helping Hurts: How to Alleviate Poverty without Hurting the Poor . . . and Yourself.* Chicago: Moody Publishers, 2014.

Schneider, John R. *The Good of Affluence: Seeking God in a Culture of Wealth.* Grand Rapids: Eerdmans, 2002.

Self, Charlie. *Flourishing Churches & Communities.* Grand Rapids: Christian's Library Press, 2013.

Sherman, Amy L. *Kingdom Calling: Vocational Calling for the Common Good.* Downers Grove, IL: InterVarsity Press, 2011.

Willard, Dallas, and Gary Black. *The Divine Conspiracy Continued.* New York: HarperOne, 2014.

Wong, Kenman, and Scott Rae. *Business for the Common Good: A Christian Vision for the Marketplace.* Downers Grove, IL: IVP Academic, 2011.

Wright, David. *How God Makes the World a Better Place: A Wesleyan Primer on Faith, Work, and Economic Transformation.* Grand Rapids: Christian's Library Press, 2013.

Economics and Work on the Margins: Remembering the Poor and the Powerless

Julius Walls

Biography

Julius Walls (BS, Concordia University) is pastor of Metropolitan A.M.E. Zion Church in Yonkers, New York, and president of Greater Centennial Community Development Corp., the nonprofit arm of a 5,000-member church. Julius has worked in business, academia, and the church, serving also as chief of staff of Greater Centennial Church, CEO of Greyston Bakery, a $7 million social enterprise, as vice president for a $23 million chocolate manufacturing company, and as an adjunct professor at the business graduate schools at NYU and BGI. He also serves on several local and national nonprofit and government boards. He is coauthor with Kevin Lynch of *Mission Inc.: The Practitioner's Guide to Social Enterprise.*

Presentation Summary

The economic machine that is America continues to move forward but continues to leave behind those who do not have an opportunity to get aboard. So while the Dow Jones rages toward higher heights, the poor and powerless fall to lower lows. But a solution both obvious and obscure exists: business. Business changes the lives of the less fortunate when leaders and shareholders look beyond their own pockets. Learn the principles of how the social enterprise of Greyston taps into the power of business to change individuals, families, and the neighborhood in Yonkers. Deuteronomy 10:18 tells us that God administers justice for the fatherless and the widow, and he loves strangers, giving them food and clothing. It then tells us to do the same.

Video Presentation: http://bit.ly/FAWS14Walls

Discussion Questions

1. Are there systemic issues in our structures that stand in the way of progress for some? What can we do about this?

2. Can a perceptually unethical model of for-profit business yield a God-desired result?

3. Does the "double bottom line" really work? Is it sustainable?

4. In what ways can we be more evenhanded in dealing with economic issues for the benefit of all in society? What is the role of trust in extending benefits to others?

5. Identify some lessons we can learn from Julius's examples that could be applied in other communities. In what ways could you participate in this work?

Resources

Eggers, William D. *The Solution Revolution: How Business, Government, and Social Enterprises Are Teaming Up to Solve Society's Toughest Problems*. Cambridge, MA: Harvard Business Review Press, 2013.

Lane, Marc J. *Social Enterprise: Empowering Mission-Driven Entrepreneurs*. Chicago: American Bar Association, 2012.

Walls, Julius Jr., and Kevin Lynch. *Mission, Inc.: A Practitioner's Guide to Social Enterprise*. Oakland, CA: Berrett-Koehler Publishers, 2009.

Part 5: Work and Faith Pioneers

A clear decline in the connection between work and faith happened among Christians near the end of the nineteenth century. Then about twenty-five years ago, interest and recognition of what the Bible has to say about this area began to grow. But even through the period between these points, many faithful Christians understood the message of the whole gospel and lived it out in business, the academy, the church, and parachurch areas. These pioneers laid the groundwork for the modern movement of faith and work, for which all of us should be grateful.

When we planned the summit, we thought it would be helpful to recognize some of these pioneers. We didn't have a scientific way of selecting who should be recognized or who were the most deserving. Rather, we picked five people whose influence had significant impact on us.

Four were business leaders who had a practical venue for working out the connection between their faith and their work "on the ground." They did this with a skill and a passion that not only influenced other Christians in the workplace but also countless people in their organizations and communities:

- **Thomas L. Phillips**, longtime chair and CEO of Raytheon

- **Howard E. Butt**, vice chair, HEB grocery chain in Texas

- **Wayne Alderson**, executive leader, Pittron Steel

- **R. G. LeTourneau**, founder of an earthmoving company

Pete Hammond, our fifth pioneer selection, is a longtime leader at InterVarsity Christian Fellowship. Early in his career, he saw the connection between faith and work, and became an encourager to students, student leaders, churches, and seminaries.

All of these leaders blazed a path with far less support than is available today, and everyone in the modern movement has some debt to them and can learn from them.

In discussing the following presentations, there are some common questions that should be considered for all of them, which follow on the next page. We have also added two questions specific to the individual pioneers whose careers are sketched out in the presentations.

Discussion Questions Common for All Tributes

1. Why do you think it might have been more difficult for these leaders to develop their own connections between their work and their faith in their time?

2. In this day when there are so many more resources for supporting the connection between work and faith than was true in their day, what are your resources?

- Books?

- Podcasts?

- Support organizations?

- Colleagues?

3. In what ways are you a resource for others, especially for the next generation?

Work and Faith Pioneer: Thomas L. Phillips

Andy Mills

Pioneer Biography

Thomas Phillips (b. 1924) served as CEO and chair of Raytheon Corporation for more than fifty years. He was also cofounder of Ethics & Compliance Officers Association, and a board member of Gordon College, SRA International, Digital Equipment, John Hancock, Knight-Ridder, State Street Bank, and Massachusetts General. Tom was also a First Tuesday Business Leader Breakfast host for the Marketplace Ministry Network, Theology of Work Project.

Presenter

Andy Mills is executive chair and president of Archegos Capital Management LP, and cochair of the Grace and Mercy Foundation. He is the former CEO of the Thomson Financial and Professional Publishing unit of the Thomson Corporation. He is the cochair of the Theology of Work Project and a senior fellow at The King's College in New York City, where he previously served as president and chair of the board of trustees.

Video Presentation: http://bit.ly/FAWS14Phillips

Discussion Questions

1. How did Tom Phillips use the platform God gave him to advance the cause of the work and faith movement? What can you learn about using your own platform?

2. How did character affect Tom Phillips in his work and walk of faith? What does this mean for those who follow?

Work and Faith Pioneer: Howard E. Butt

Mark Roberts

Pioneer Biography

Howard Butt (b. 1927) was the vice chair of H. E. Butt Grocery Company and president of H. E. Butt Foundation, Laity Renewal Foundation, and Laity Lodge Foundation. The radio voice of "High Calling of Our Daily Work," Howard authored *At the Edge of Hope: Christian Laity in Paradox*, *The Velvet Covered Brick: Christian Leadership in an Age of Rebellion*, and other works. He was also a board member for *Christianity Today* and the Billy Graham Evangelistic Association.

Presenter

Mark D. Roberts is executive director for the Max De Pree Center for Leadership at Fuller Theological Seminary, where he is the principal writer of the *Life for Leaders* daily devotional and a major contributor to the *Insights for Leaders* blog of the De Pree Center. Previously, Mark was executive director of digital media and senior director of the Laity Lodge retreat center. Earlier, he served as senior pastor of Irvine Presbyterian Church in Southern California. Mark has written several books, including *Can We Trust the Gospels?* and *Discovering Advent: How to Experience the Power of Waiting on God at Christmastime*.

Video Presentation: http://bit.ly/FAWS14HButt

Discussion Questions

1. What factors led to Howard Butt's career transition from evangelist to the marketplace? What can you learn from this transition for your own career?

2. How did Howard's struggle with depression affect his interests in the connection between work and faith? How does this challenge us to see the faith and work movement in a bigger context?

Work and Faith Pioneer: Wayne Alderson

Albert M. Erisman

Biography

Wayne Alderson (1926–2013) was the founder of Value of the Person Seminars, former vice president of Pittron Steel and Labor's Man of the Year in Pennsylvania (the only management person so honored); he received a Purple Heart and a Bronze Star for his service during World War II. He was author (with Nancy Alderson McDonnell) of *Theory R Management* and the subject of the biography, *Stronger Than Steel* by R. C. Sproul. The film on his work, *Miracle at Pittron*, inspired many in the faith at work movement.

Presenter

Albert M. Erisman (BS, Northern Illinois University; MS, PhD, Iowa State University) is executive in residence at the Seattle Pacific University School of Business, Government, and Economics. He also cochairs the Theology of Work Project (www.theologyofwork.org) and cofounded and edits *Ethix* magazine (www.ethix.org). He previously served as a senior technical fellow and director of R&D in technology and mathematics at The Boeing Company (1969–2001). He is author or editor of six books, including *Direct Methods for Sparse Matrices* with I. S. Duff and J. K. Reid (Oxford: Clarendon Press, 1989), *The Purpose of Business*, and *The Accidental Executive: Lessons on Business, Faith, and Calling from the Life of Joseph*.

Video Presentation: http://bit.ly/FAWS14Alderson

Discussion Questions

1. How did early influences in Wayne's life in his home, in the service, and at Pittron Steel together shape his approach to management and labor? How did his application of "God has given us the ministry of reconciliation" change the way he did his work? What can you learn from this?

2. What did it mean for Wayne to value people in the workplace? In what ways can we learn from him in this area?

Work and Faith Pioneer: R. G. LeTourneau

Bill Peel

Biography

R. G. LeTourneau (1888–1969) was a prolific inventor (with nearly 300 patents) of earthmoving machinery, and during World War II, LeTourneau machines supplied nearly 70 percent of the earthmoving equipment and engineering vehicles used. He also founded LeTourneau University in Texas, and served both CBMC and Gideons as president. Widely known as "God's businessman," LeTourneau wrote *Mover of Men and Mountains*, which has been used by many in business as a foundation for their own work.

Presenter

Bill Peel (BA, Southern Methodist University; ThM, Dallas Theological Seminary; DMin, Gordon-Conwell Theological Seminary) is the founding executive director of the Center for Faith & Work at LeTourneau University (www.centerforfaithandwork.com). For more than thirty years, Bill has coached thousands of men and women to discover their calling, understand their work's significance to God, and become spiritually influential in their workplace. He is an award-winning author of seven books (available in multiple languages), including *Workplace Grace* and *What God Does When Men Pray*.

Video Presentation: http://bit.ly/FAWS14LeTourneau

Discussion Questions

1. Why did R. G. LeTourneau go into business rather than to the mission field? How do we face and resolve similar challenges?

2. How did he use engineering skills to honor God? What skill set do you bring to your work in the marketplace, and how might these skills be used to God's glory?

Work and Faith Pioneer: Pete Hammond

John Terrill

Pioneer Biography

Pete Hammond (1936–2008) was an InterVarsity Christian Fellowship staff member and leader for forty-one years. He was also a pioneer of IVCF marketplace ministry and worked as a farmer, carpenter, coach, teacher, rodeo cowboy, and adjunct seminary professor. He served as creative developer of *Word and Faith Study Bible*, coauthored *Marketplace Annotated Bibliography*, was the catalyst and founder of the Mockler Center, and was a board member of Presbyterians for Renewal, Bellhaven College, and *Christianity Today*.

Presenter

John Terrill serves as executive director of the Stephen & Laurel Brown Foundation. Prior to this role, John served as director for the Center for Integrity in Business at the School of Business, Government, and Economics at Seattle Pacific University. Prior to Seattle Pacific, John worked with InterVarsity Christian Fellowship as the national director for Professional Schools Ministries, as well as campus minister at Harvard Business School and national director for MBA Ministry. Before InterVarsity, John consulted with Hay Group, an international management consulting firm.

Video Presentation: http://bit.ly/FAWS14Hammond

Discussion Questions

1. How did Pete Hammond's unique background affect his role in the work and faith movement? What from your own background might be used to turn challenges into opportunities?

2. How did Pete connect the issues of work and faith with the issues of racial justice? How do you see these issues tied together?

Litany of Commitment

Bill Peel

Affirmation: Holy Trinity, we marvel at the universe you worked together to create. The whole universe is your temple, a place of worship, in which you called us to join your work in bringing creation to full flower.

> *We are grateful for your high calling to participate in your work. Whatever good endeavor our hands find to do, no matter how mundane, help us to recognize that you want it done, done well, and as an act of love for you and our neighbor. May our daily work echo praise to you as much as singing a hymn.[1]*

Father, thank you for the beauty and bounty of creation. Every square inch of it belongs to you.

> *May we enjoy what you've given us and steward it well, knowing that we will give account to you for how we use it. Prosper us, Lord, so we may be exceptionally generous and bless others in significant ways. Enable us to create good jobs so those who need work can experience the dignity of meeting their own needs and have enough to share with others as their cup overflows.[2]*

Lord Jesus, you promised that the Holy Spirit would lead us into all truth and empower us to apply it more fully in our lives.

> *Instill in us a holy desire to want what you want and to love what you love—that we may love and serve others well through our work and be a fragrant aroma of Christ to all.*

---

[1] Genesis 1–2; 1 Thessalonians 4:11
[2] Genesis 1:27–28; Ephesians 4:28; 1 Thessalonians 4:11

May our work reflect your character, remind people of your presence, and may your Spirit draw thousands to Christ through the witness of your church in the workplace.[3]

Father, thank you for your commitment to make us like your Son. Through your Son we have been blessed with every spiritual blessing. We lack nothing to do your will.

Deliver us from any sense of scarcity that breeds greed. Help us to exercise integrity in everything we do, and lead us to recognize and repent of any practice, no matter how convenient or profitable, that cannot be done in your name and for your glory.[4]

Lord Jesus, thank you for your presence and the courage and stamina you give us to stand up against temptation, trials, and persecution as we seek to imitate you in all we do.

So captivate our hearts with your grace that there be no room left for anything that dishonors you. Empower us to forgive as we are forgiven and be pure and gentle in everything we do, knowing that we have a Master in Heaven.[5]

Holy Spirit, thank you for the talents and abilities with which you have blessed us. We recognize that they are gifts from your generous hand. Whatever we possess comes from you, not from our own strength, savvy, or smarts. They belong to you and are to be used to for your glory.

Keep us from the self-deception and rationalization that leads us to think more highly of ourselves than we ought. Forgive us for seeking to make a name for ourselves, taking rather than giving, and seeking to be served rather

---

[3] Romans 12:9–21; 2 Corinthians 2:15
[4] Matthew 5:16; Romans 8:29
[5] John 15:20; Ephesians 5:18; Colossians 3:15; 1 Peter 5:6–11

than to serve. Help us to lead with humility and do our work with diligence and craftsmanship so that we, our coworkers, and our community may flourish.[6]

Father, thank you that you have not left us to live and work alone but made us members of your body and of one another, gifting us and placing us just where you know best.

Forgive us, Lord, for ever thinking we don't need others, or holding back, thinking that others don't need us. Help us, Lord, to work together in the unity of the Spirit and the bond of peace so the world will know you are real.[7]

Father, thank you for the opportunity to gather as your church. We thank you for our pastors and spiritual leaders who equip us to serve you seven days a week.

We ask that your Spirit would give them wisdom and clarity as they lead, teach, and prepare us to do our work as an act of service to others and for your glory when we go to our places in the ministry of our daily work.[8]

Father, we thank you for entrusting us with roles of leadership and placing us in arenas of influence.

We ask that you raise up pastors and business leaders around the globe to work together to multiply spiritual leaders in the workplace who will live out their calling to your glory. Use us to mentor and develop leaders for the future who will carry the gospel to the next generations.[9]

---

[6] Proverbs 22:29; Jeremiah 29:7; Romans 12:3–8; Ephesians 2:10; 6:9; Colossians 3:22–4:1

[7] Genesis 2:18; 2 Corinthians 12:1–31; John 17:1–26

[8] Ephesians 4:11–16; Hebrews 10:24–25

[9] 2 Timothy 2:2

In all we do, Father, in every area of our lives, may we bring glory and honor to your name.

Created for the Faith@Work Summit, Boston, October 2014

Bibliography

Alderson, Wayne, and Nancy Alderson McDonnell. *Theory R Management*. Nashville: Thomas Nelson, 1994.

Beckett, John. *Mastering Monday: A Guide to Integrating Faith & Work*. Downers Grove, IL: InterVarsity Press, 2006.

Blackaby, Henry, Richard Blackaby, and Claude King. *Experiencing God: Knowing and Doing the Will of God*. Nashville: B&H Books, 2008.

Bloom, Sandra L. *Creating Sanctuary: Toward the Evolution of Sane Societies*. London: Routledge, 2013.

Boland, John W. *Workplace Evangelism: Taking Your Faith to Work*. Mustang, OK: Tate Publishing, 2013.

Bolt, John. *Economic Shalom: A Reformed Primer on Faith, Work, and Human Flourishing*. Grand Rapids: Christian Library Press, 2013.

Brende, Eric. *Better Off: Flipping the Switch on Technology*. New York: Harper Perennial, 2005.

Briner, Robert. *Roaring Lambs: A Gentle Plan to Radically Change Your World*. Grand Rapids: Zondervan, 1995.

Brown, Peter. *Through the Eye of a Needle: Wealth, the Fall of Rome, and the Making of Christianity in the West, 350–550 AD*. Princeton: Princeton University Press, 2014.

Buford, Bob. *Drucker and Me: What a Texas Entrepreneur Learned from the Father of Modern Management*. Franklin, TN: Worthy Publishing, 2007.

Butt, Howard E. *At the Edge of Hope: Christian Laity in Paradox*. New York: Seabury Press, 1978.

———. *The Velvet Covered Brick: Christian Leadership in an Age of Rebellion*. New York: Harper & Row, 1973.

Carey, George, and Andrew Carey. *We Don't Do God: The Marginalization of Public Faith*. Oxford: Monarch Books, 2012.

Charan, Ram. *Global Tilt: Leading Your Business through the Great Economic Power Shift*. New York: Crown Business, 2013.

Claar, Victor, and Robin Klay. *Economics in Christian Perspective: Theory, Policy and Life Choices.* Downers Grove, IL: InterVarsity Press, 2007.

Cleveland, Drew, and Greg Foster, eds. *The Pastor's Guide to Fruitful Work and Economic Wisdom: Understanding What Your People Do All Day.* Overland Park, KS: Made to Flourish, 2012.

Corbett, Steve, and Brian Fikkert. *When Helping Hurts: How to Alleviate Poverty without Hurting the Poor . . . and Yourself.* Chicago: Moody Publishers, 2014.

Cosden, Darrell. *The Heavenly Good of Earthly Work.* Grand Rapids: Baker Academic, 2006.

———. *A Theology of Work: Work and the New Creation.* Eugene, OR: Wipf & Stock Publications, 2004.

Crouch, Andy. *Culture Making: Recovering Our Creative Calling.* Downers Grove, IL: InterVarsity Press, 2008.

DeKoster, Lester. *Work: The Meaning of Your Life; A Christian Perspective.* Grand Rapids: Acton Institute, 2010.

DeMillo, Richard A. *Abelard to Apple: The Fate of American Colleges and Universities.* New York: Jossey-Bass, 2011.

De Soto, Hernando. *The Mystery of Capital: Why Capitalism Succeeds in the West and Fails Everywhere Else.* New York: Basic Books, 2003.

Dunn, Richard R., and Jana L. Sundene. *Shaping the Journey of Emerging Adults: Life-Giving Rhythms for Spiritual Transformation.* Downers Grove, IL: InterVarsity Press, 2012.

Dyer, John. *From the Garden to the City: The Redeeming and Corrupting Power of Technology.* Grand Rapids: Kregel Publications, 2011.

Eggers, William D. *The Solution Revolution: How Business, Government, and Social Enterprises Are Teaming Up to Solve Society's Toughest Problems.* Cambridge, MA: Harvard Business Review Press, 2013.

Eldred, Ken. *God Is at Work: Transforming People and Nations through Business.* Grand Rapids: Regal Books, 2005.

Ellul, Jacques. *The Presence of the Kingdom.* Colorado Springs: Helmers & Howard, 1989.

Erisman, Albert M. *The Accidental Executive: Lessons on Business, Faith, and Calling from the Life of Joseph.* Peabody, MA: Hendrickson, 2015.

Erisman, Albert M., and David Gautschi, eds. *The Purpose of Business: Contemporary Perspectives from Different Walks of Life.* London: Palgrave Macmillan, 2015.

Evans, Alice Frazer, Robert A. Evans, and William Bean Kennedy. *Pedagogies for the Non-Poor.* Maryknoll: Orbis Books, 1987.

Flake, Floyd, and Donna Marie Williams. *The Way of the Bootstrapper: Nine Action Steps for Achieving Your Dreams.* New York: Amistad, 2000.

Garber, Steve. *The Fabric of Faithfulness: Weaving Together Belief and Behavior.* Downers Grove, IL: InterVarsity Press, 2007.

———. *Visions of Vocation: Common Grace for the Common Good.* Downers Grove, IL: InterVarsity Press, 2014.

Gill, David W. *Becoming Good: Building Moral Character.* Downers Grove, IL: InterVarsity Press, 2000.

———. *Doing Right: Practicing Ethical Principles.* Downers Grove, IL: InterVarsity Press, 2004.

———. *It's About Excellence: Building Ethically Healthy Organizations.* Eugene, OR: Wipf & Stock, 2011.

Goosen, Richard J., and R. Paul Stevens. *Entrepreneurial Leadership: Finding Your Calling, Making a Difference.* Downers Grove, IL: InterVarsity Press, 2013.

Greenleaf, Robert. *Servant Leadership: A Journey into the Nature of Legitimate Power and Greatness.* New York: Paulist Press, 1991.

Greer, Peter, and Chris Horst. *Entrepreneurship for Human Flourishing.* Washington, DC: AEI Press, 2014.

Grudem, Wayne. *Business for the Glory of God: The Bible's Teaching on the Moral Goodness of Business.* Wheaton, IL: Crossway, 2003.

Grudem, Wayne, and Barry Asmus. *The Poverty of Nations: A Sustainable Solution*. Wheaton, IL: Crossway, 2013.

Guillebeau, Chris. *The $100 Start-Up: Reinvent the Way You Make a Living, Do What You Love, and Create a New Future*. New York: Crown Business, 2012.

Gwartney, James D., Richard L. Stroup, Dwight R. Lee, and Tawni Hunt Ferrarini. *Common Sense Economics: What Everyone Should Know About Wealth and Prosperity*. New York: St. Martin's Press, 2010.

Hammond, Pete, and Bill Hendricks. *Word in Life Study Bible*. Nashville: Thomas Nelson, 1993.

Hammond, Pete, R. Paul Stevens, and Todd Svanoe. *Marketplace Annotated Bibliography: A Christian Guide to Books on Work, Business and Vocation*. Downers Grove, IL: InterVarsity Press, 2002.

Hawken, Paul. *Blessed Unrest: How the Largest Social Movement in the World Came into Being and Why No One Saw It Coming*. London: Penguin Books, 2007.

Hillman, Os. *Faith@Work*. Fairfield, CT: Aslan Publishing, 2004.

Hopper, Kenneth, and William Hopper. *The Puritan Gift: Triumph, Collapse and Revival of an American Dream*. London: Palgrave Macmillan, 2007.

Hunter, James Davidson. *To Change the World: The Irony, Tragedy, and Possibility of Christianity in the Late Modern World*. Oxford: Oxford University Press, 2010.

Hyun, Jane, and Audrey S. Lee. *Flex: The New Playbook for Managing Across Differences*. New York: HarperBusiness, 2014.

Jenkins, Philip. *The Next Christendom: The Coming of Global Christianity*. Oxford: Oxford University Press, 2011.

Jones, Laurie Beth. *Jesus, CEO: Using Ancient Wisdom for Visionary Leadership*. New York: Hachette Books, 1996.

Kawasaki, Guy. *The Art of the Start: The Time-Tested, Battle-Hardened Guide for Anyone Starting Anything*. London: Penguin/Portfolio, 2004.

Keller, Timothy. *Counterfeit Gods: The Empty Promises of Money, Sex, and Power, and the Only Hope That Matters.* New York: Viking, 2009.

———. *The Reason for God: Belief in an Age of Skepticism.* New York: Viking, 2008.

Keller, Timothy, with Katherine Leary Alsdorf. *Every Good Endeavor: Connecting Your Work to God's Work.* New York: Dutton Adult, 2012.

Khurana, Rakesh. *From Higher Aims to Hired Hands: The Social Transformation of American Business Schools and the Unfulfilled Promise of Management as a Profession.* Princeton: Princeton University Press, 2007.

Kim, David H. *20 and Something: Have the Time of Your Life (And Figure It All Out Too).* Grand Rapids: Zondervan, 2014.

Kraemer, Hendrik. *A Theology of the Laity.* Louisville, KY: Westminster Press, 1958.

Lane, Marc J. *Social Enterprise: Empowering Mission-Driven Entrepreneurs.* Chicago: American Bar Association, 2012.

Larive, Armand E. *After Sunday: A Theology of Work.* London: Bloomsbury Academic, 2004.

Lee, Jean. *Two Pillars of the Market: A Paradigm for Dialogue between Theology and Economics.* New York: Lang, 2011.

LeTourneau, R. G. *Mover of Men and Mountains.* Chicago: Moody Publishers, 1967.

Maciarello, Joseph, and Karen Linkletter. *Drucker's Lost Art of Management: Peter Drucker's Timeless Vision for Building Effective Organizations.* New York: McGraw-Hill Education, 2011.

MacIntyre, Alasdair. *After Virtue: A Study in Moral Theory.* 2nd ed. South Bend, IN: University of Notre Dame Press, 1984.

———. *Three Rival Versions of Moral Enquiry: Encyclopedia, Genealogy & Tradition.* South Bend, IN: University of Notre Dame Press, 1990.

Messenger, William, ed. *Theology of Work Bible Commentary.* Peabody, MA: Hendrickson, 2016.

Miller, David W. *God at Work: The History and Promise of the Faith at Work Movement.* Oxford: Oxford University Press, 2006.

Mitroff, Ian, and Elizabeth Denton. *A Spiritual Audit of Corporate America: A Hard Look at Spirituality, Religion, and Values in the Workplace.* New York: Wiley & Sons, 1999.

Nash, Laura and Scotty McLennan. *Church on Sunday, Work on Monday: The Challenge of Fusing Christian Values with Business Life.* New York: Jossey-Bass, 2001.

Nelson, Tom. *Ekklesia: Rediscovering God's Design for the Church.* Grand Island, NE: Cross Training Publishing, 2010.

———. *Five Smooth Stones: Discovering the Path to Wholeness of Soul.* Grand Island, NE: Cross Training Publishing, 2001.

———. *Work Matters: Connecting Sunday Worship to Monday Work.* Wheaton, IL: Crossway, 2011.

Nicholl, Armand. *The Question of God: C. S. Lewis and Sigmund Freud Debate God, Love, Sex, and the Meaning of Life.* Glencoe, IL: Free Press, 2003.

Novak, Michael. *Business as a Calling: Work and the Examined Life.* Glencoe, IL: Free Press, 2013.

Peel, Bill. *What God Does When Men Pray: A Small-Group Discussion Guide.* Colorado Springs: NavPress, 2014.

Peel, Bill, and Walt Larimore. *Grace Prescriptions.* Bristol, TN: Christian Medical & Dental Associations, 2014.

———. *Workplace Grace: Becoming a Spiritual Influence in the Workplace.* Longview, TX: LeTourneau University Press, 2014.

Pollard, C. William. *Serving Two Masters? Reflections on God and Profit.* New York: HarperCollins, 2006.

———. *The Soul of the Firm.* New York: HarperBusiness, 2010.

———. *The Tides of Life: Learning to Lead and Serve as You Navigate the Currents of Life.* Wheaton, IL: Crossway, 2014.

Powers, William. *Hamlet's BlackBerry: A Practical Philosophy for Building a Good Life in the Digital Age.* New York: Harper. 2010.

Roberts, Mark. *Can We Trust the Gospels? Investigating the Reliability of Matthew, Mark, Luke, and John.* Wheaton, IL: Crossway, 2007.

————. *Discovering Advent: How to Experience the Power of Waiting on God at Christmastime*. Denver: Patheos, 2011.

Russell, Mark L., and Dave Gibbons. *Our Souls at Work*. London: Russell Media, 2010.

Schneider, John. *The Good of Affluence: Seeking God in a Culture of Wealth*. Grand Rapids: Eerdmans, 2002.

Self, Charlie. *Flourishing Churches & Communities*. Grand Rapids: Christian's Library Press, 2013.

Selingo, Jeffrey. *College Unbound: The Future of Higher Education and What It Means for Students*. New York: Houghton-Mifflin, 2013.

Shannahan, Chris. *Voices from the Borderland: Re-Imagining Cross-Cultural Urban Theology in the Twenty-First Century*. London: Equinox, 2010.

Sherman, Amy L. *Kingdom Calling: Vocational Stewardship for the Common Good*. Downers Grove, IL: InterVarsity Press, 2011.

Sherman, Doug, and William Hendricks. *Your Work Matters to God*. Colorado Springs: NavPress, 1990.

Silvoso, Ed. *Anointed for Business: How to Use Your Influence in the Marketplace to Change the World*. New York: Regal Books, 2006.

Simpson, Michael L. *Permission Evangelism: When to Talk, When to Walk*. Colorado Springs: Cook Communications, 2003.

Smith, David. *Mission after Christendom*. London: Darton, Longman & Todd, 2003.

Solomon, Robert. *A Better Way to Think About Business Ethics: How Personal Integrity Leads to Corporate Success*. Oxford: Oxford University Press, 1999.

Sowell, Thomas. *Basic Economics: A Common Sense Guide to the Economy*. New York: Basic Books, 2007.

Spada, Doug, and Dave Scott. *Monday Morning Atheist: Why We Switch God Off at Work and How You Fix It*. McKenny, TX: Worklife Press, 2012.

Sproul, R. C. *Stronger Than Steel: The Wayne Alderson Story*. New York: Harper & Row, 1980.

Stevens, R. Paul. *Work Matters: Lessons from Scripture*. Grand Rapids: Eerdmans, 2012.

Stiglitz, Joseph E. *Making Globalization Work*. New York: W. W. Norton, 2006.

Traeger, Sebastian, and Greg Gilbert. *The Gospel at Work: How Working for King Jesus Gives Purpose and Meaning to Our Jobs*. Grand Rapids: Zondervan, 2014.

Van Duzer, Jeff. *Why Business Matters to God (And What Still Needs to Be Fixed)*. Downers Grove, IL: InterVarsity Press, 2010.

Walls, Julius Jr., and Kevin Lynch. *Mission Inc.: A Practitioner's Guide to Social Enterprise*. Oakland, CA: Berrett-Koehler Publishers, 2009.

Wheatley, Margaret J. *Finding Our Way: Leadership for an Uncertain Time*. Oakland, CA: Berrett-Koehler Publisher, 2005.

Whelchel, Hugh. *How Then Should We Work? Rediscovering the Biblical Doctrine of Work*. Wheaton, IL: WestBow, 2012.

Willard, Dallas, and Gary Black. *The Divine Conspiracy Continued*. New York: HarperOne, 2014.

Witherington III, Ben. *Work: A Kingdom Perspective on Labor*. Grand Rapids: Eerdmans, 2011.

Wolters, Albert M. *Creation Regained: Biblical Basis for a Reformational Worldview*. Grand Rapids: Eerdmans, 2005.

Wong, Kenman, and Scott Rae. *Business for the Common Good: A Christian Vision for the Marketplace*. Downers Grove, IL: InterVarsity Press, 2011.

Wright, David. *How God Makes the World a Better Place: A Wesleyan Primer on Faith, Work, and Economic Transformation*. Grand Rapids: Christian Library Press, 2013.

Wuthnow, Robert. *America and the Challenges of Religious Diversity*. Princeton: Princeton University Press, 2005.

Yunus, Muhammad. *Banker to the Poor: Micro-Lending and the Battle against World Poverty*. New York: PublicAffairs, 2003.

Ziglar, Zig. *Better Than Good: Creating a Life You Can't Wait to Live*. Nashville: Thomas Nelson, 2007.

About the Hendrickson Publishers/ Theology of Work Line of Books

There is an unprecedented interest today in the role of Christian faith in "ordinary" work, and Christians in every field are exploring what it means to work "as to the Lord" (Col. 3:22). Pastors and church leaders, and the scholars and teachers who support them, are asking what churches can do to equip their members in the workplace. There's a need for deep thinking, fresh perspectives, practical ideas, and mutual engagement between Christian faith and work in every sphere of human endeavor.

This Hendrickson Publishers/Theology of Work line of books seeks to bring significant new resources into this conversation. It began with Hendrickson's publication of the *Theology of Work Bible Commentary* and other Bible study materials written by the TOW Project. Soon we discovered a wealth of resources by other writers with a common heart for the meaning and value of everyday work. The HP/TOW line was formed to make the best of these resources available on the national and international stage.

Works in the HP/TOW line engage the practical issues of daily work through the lens of the Bible and the other resources of the Christian faith. They are biblically grounded, but their subjects are the work, workers, and workplaces of today. They employ contemporary arts and sciences, best practices, empirical research, and wisdom gained from experience, yet always in the service of Christ's redemptive work in the world, especially the world of work.

To a greater or lesser degree, all the books in this line make use of the scholarship of the *Theology of Work Bible Commentary*. The authors, however, are not limited to the TOW Project's perspectives, and they constantly expand the scope and application of the material. Publication of a book in the HP/TOW line does not necessarily imply endorsement by the Theology of Work Project, or that the author endorses the TOW Project. It does mean we recognize the work as an important contribution to the faith-work discussion, and we find a common footing that makes us glad to walk side-by-side in the dialogue.

We are proud to present the HP/TOW line together. We hope it helps readers expand their thinking, explore ideas worthy of deeper thought, and make sense of their own work in light of the Christian faith. We are grateful to the authors and all those whose labor has brought the HP/TOW line to life.

William Messenger, Executive Editor, Theology of Work Project
Sean McDonough, Biblical Editor, Theology of Work Project
Patricia Anders, Editorial Director, Hendrickson Publishers

www.theologyofwork.org
www.hendrickson.com

"This commentary was written exactly for those of us who aim to integrate our faith and work on a daily basis and is an excellent reminder that God hasn't called the world to go to the church, but has called the Church to go to the world."

BONNIE WURZBACHER

FORMER SENIOR VICE PRESIDENT, THE COCA-COLA COMPANY

HENDRICKSON
PUBLISHERS   THEOLOGY OF WORK   PROJECT